love

THROUGHOUT

MISTI GIL

love
THROUGHOUT

A Study of God's Multifaceted Love

FROM GENESIS TO REVELATION

FEATHERED ANCHOR PUBLISHING

LOVE THROUGHOUT

For Jesus

This is the firstfruits of my book writing labor,

and it is my pleasure to give it back to you.

Thank you for your love

that sees me through

every season.

acknowledgments

Lou – You have taught me what it looks like to love with no strings attached. You continually give of yourself to me, Cooper and your Young Life kids with very little thought for yourself. You inspire me, and I pray I will someday be able to love as fully as you do. You truly are the hands and feet of Jesus to our community here in this little slice of Texas. I'm proud to be your wife, I'm enjoying getting to know you better after all these years of marriage, and I adore you in a gross-out-your-children kind of way.

Cooper – I learned a completely new kind of love when I held you in my arms for the first time. I know I tell you year four was my favorite stage, but, really, every age you've ever been has been the best. I just love being your mom, man. You bring me a joy I never knew I could have, and watching you grow up and learn to love Jesus and people is my greatest honor. Thank you for being the best teenager around. Don't tell any of the others, but you're my favorite. I love you, bud.

Team Awesome – Candus and Mom, wow! I have no idea how to even thank you for everything you've done. You've listened to my endless ideas and aimless chattering, talked me off ledges, encouraged me, challenged me, taken over the parts of ministry that drive me nuts and provided me with every type of help I could ever need. Candus – you might be one of the most selfless people I know. Who pays a person's salary for an entire year just so that person can have space to pursue her dream? You do! Thank you for financially backing this year of writing and for refusing to let me think I'm less than amazing. Thank you for being faithful to always give me a metaphorical slap upside the head when I feel like I can't do something. Your belief in me and your Can Do Mentality move me forward and help keep me from giving up on my dream. I not only love you, I genuinely like you as a person. Mom, your prayers are integral to my sanity. The talks we've had about God, His purpose for me and how I absolutely can walk in the calling He's given me have been the buoy I need in the crazy sea of full-time ministry. You have believed in me and been my constant voice of encouragement and confidence for as long as I can remember. You have always been my safe person – the one I absolutely KNOW will listen for as long as I talk, respond in love and point me back to Jesus. I'm so glad God gave me you to mother me. You're perfect for me, and you've become one of my very best friends. Thank you both from the depth of my soul. I will never be able to repay you, but I will try. You guys have loved me well. I love you both so, so much.

Dad – Thank you for always being there for me. I've known since the days I donned pigtails that you've got my back. You always take care of your girls and are dependable, trustworthy, giving and happy to spend your time with us. Thank you for modeling those attributes of Christ for me in such a way that it helped me believe that my God could also be dependable, trustworthy, giving and excited to be with me. I love you.

Aimee, Ashley, Kiki – Talk about pulling me off a ledge! As my best friends, you also have the unenviable task of being my free counselors. I must owe you thousands of dollars in back payment. Thank you for loving God enough to speak truth to me and gift me with beautiful, deep, fun friendship. It sustains me some days. I love you all so, so much.

Mary Beth – You have always believed in my writing and been one of my biggest cheerleaders. Thank you for your constant encouragement and for being the first to buy this book! Boom! Love you, boo!

Linda – Thank you for your spiritual guidance during this time. You have led me to the feet of Jesus and shown me how to love well with the gifts God gives us. You have also been instrumental in helping me discern His call. I love you.

My FWA kids –Thank you for your excitement for this project and for being a joy to be around every time I see your faces. Part of my journey to begin writing a Bible study was a direct result of you thinking I'm a pretty good teacher. I love you all so much. Come visit me!

Mary DeMuth – You are a wealth of book writing and publishing knowledge. Thank you for everything you've taught me along this journey and your sweet words about my writing ability and publishing potential. You are a sweet friend and a wise counselor.

Kelly Drose – I cannot believe this book cover is your first. You're gifted, girl, and I love that you're using your talents to serve the kingdom. Thank you for the Love Throughout cover; it's beautiful.

Beth Moore – Beth, I have been attending your classes and Bible studies for two decades now, and God used you to bring me into a relationship with Himself. As I sat in your Sunday school classes and Tuesday night studies at Houston's First Baptist Church, I saw a light and joy I had never experienced. And I wanted it. Thank you for loving Jesus so richly that those around you can see it and ask Him to do the same in them. Thank you for teaching truth. You don't know me, but I love you. I just made it weird, didn't I?

Emily P Freeman, Jennie Allen, Shauna Niequist and Chris Hodges – Thank you for *Grace for the Good Girl, Nothing to Prove, Present over Perfect and Fresh Air*. As I spent hours in your words, I experienced a shift from Law Follower to Love Receiver. That shift led me into the beginning stages of this study. Thank you for the hard work and faithfulness it took to pen the lessons God taught you so we can all learn them too. They changed me.

❧ Contents ❧

NEW TESTAMENT

a note from misti

Hey, y'all! I can't even tell you how excited I am to have these brief moments with you every day to talk a bit about God's love for you. It's been a long time comin'. I'll tell you that right now.

I've walked with Jesus for 20 years now, but for the longest time, there was a gaping hole in my relationship with Him. I'm not even sure I knew it was there. All I knew was that I was showing up to church, reading my Bible, praying all the time and teaching my child about Jesus, but something wasn't right. It wasn't until over a decade later that I realized that though the idea of God's love sounded dreamy, that's exactly what it had always felt like to me: a dream. A sentiment I wish were true, but I suspected wasn't. I longed to believe all the teachers and pastors who repeatedly assured me that God adored me, but every time I felt like I messed something up, I was racked with shame: a tell-tale sign that we haven't really accepted God's love and grace fully.

I've realized many Christians feel the same. They've heard of God's love; they even believe He loves other people. But embracing it for themselves? That's a whole other story.

How about you? If I were to ask you how God feels about you, what would your first answer be? Would it be that He's crazy about you? That He thinks of you often and smiles when He does?

I have heard the Bible called God's love letter to His people. However, for years, as I read and studied it, all that seemed to register for me was God's wrath, law, rules and discipline. A checklist of things to do and not do and the punishment that might ensue if you screwed something up. Yeah, I saw scriptures about God's heart for us, but they bounced off my brain and oozed out my ears as though I had never seen the words – the Old Testament ones in particular.

Then one day I woke up empty.

A life with Jesus made up of trying to follow a shopping list of rules is exhausting and leaves you depleted, deflated and done. I hadn't given up; I did have enough juice left to not turn my back on God for good, but I was at a place where Christianity wasn't coming through on all its promises. I wasn't free. I was tired.

God then took me on a journey to find and accept His love for myself. It started as a simple daily prayer for God to show me He truly loves me – to open my eyes to all the ways He loves me every day. Up to this point I thought of the Bible as a divided sermon: the Old Testament as a picture of God's wrath and the New Testament as an illustration of His love. But in the way He does, as I read through the first 39 books of the Bible, He showed me He has never changed. He wasn't a different God in those ancient days.

God *is* love.

He loved before the cross as much as He does now, and I can't wait to show you evidence of that from every single book of the Bible – even the ones filled with His judgment.

My prayer is that as you journey with God through His word over the next two months, you would pray for Him to show you His love for YOU and that He would settle it once and for all. His word can do that.

He loves you. Always has. And that will never, ever change.

He's not only written it all over the Bible, but He's written it on your heart and on His nail-scarred hands.

Come on along with me as we search out God's heart for you from Genesis to Revelation. It will be an adventure that could change your faith forever. It did mine. Jesus, make it so.

Love to you,

Misti

❧ How To Use This Book ❧

In the Christian world, we hear a lot about having a "quiet time". I'm not fond of that phrase; I'm not sure why. Maybe because I chuck anything that reeks of putting Jesus on a checklist of things to do. Nevertheless, spending time alone with God is important, and that is usually best done in a quiet space. So, I guess the term is legit. Anyway, this Bible Study Short is designed to help you do just that in a way in which you are traveling progressively from the beginning of the Bible to the end and integrating what you read into your daily life – all in 15-30 minutes.

Every chapter begins with a "focus verse" that is centered at the top of the page. This scripture is central to our teaching, and I will refer to it periodically. Most days, I will also give you an introduction to the portion of the Bible you are about to read. As you continue to read, you will come to a scripture that *looks like this*. That is your cue to go ahead and find that scripture in your Bible or on your Bible app and read it. If you need a quick tutorial on how to look up Bible verses, I gotcha. Check the appendix.

I will then offer a few of my observations from our reading and, hopefully, give you some things to think about. Next, you will see a section titled **Pick and Pray**, where there will be three questions listed. Pick one, two or all three and pray a bit about what they're asking.

Your last section will be titled **Process**. This is simply an area filled with blank lines. This is for you to write down anything you want to remember from your scripture, reading or praying. It's a place to process what God might be saying to you. If you need more space, there are more blank pages in the back of the book. Tip: if you need to use those, write down what back pages you use at the end of that day's process section. It'll make it easier to find later.

That's it! You have freedom here. You can do one chapter a day for 66 days, one every other day for 132 days, or whatever fits *your* personality. This is not meant to shackle you to something you must do every day. It's meant to free you to experience God in whatever way He wants to reach you.

I pray as you spend regular time in God's word, your heart is changed and you walk a little lighter knowing you are deeply loved and free to walk in grace.

LOVE THROUGHOUT *the* Old Testament

REDEMPTIVE LOVE

As for you, you meant evil against me,
but God meant it for good, to bring it about that many people
should be kept alive, as they are today.
Genesis 50:20

Genesis is a book of beginnings – the beginning of the world, of God's people, of relationship, of purity and sin. You name it, and you can likely find the birth of it in the first book of the Bible. I think it only appropriate this book open with a beloved character at the beginning of his life too: Joseph – a teen with a head full of dreams and a mouth bent on impulsive oversharing.

You can find Joseph's entire story in Genesis 37 – 50, so if you are a reader, jump on in there. However, for the sake of time here, we'll do a *very* brief synopsis of details that are important to us today. Joseph was his father's most beloved son who had been told by God through dreams that he would someday rule over his family. Young Joseph, of course, thought it a good idea to share such things with his brothers, so they promptly sold him into slavery. Nice guys. After some years in an Egyptian prison for a crime he didn't commit and a curious rescue and promotion, Joseph ended up second in command over all of Egypt in his adult years. Talk about a story of riches to rags to riches!

How do you think 17-year-old Joseph felt when his brothers turned on him so heartlessly?

One would think his older siblings would possess a bit more maturity and chalk Joseph's childish self-promotion up to, well, childishness, but they did not. When I put myself in rejected Joseph's shoes as he bumped along a desert road with his brothers disappearing in the distance, all I can feel is an empty sadness. He had been hurled from the heights of the beloved down to the depths of the despised. That kind of dive can ruin a person forever.

But God was with Joseph, and that made all the difference.

God had a plan for Joseph's pain. Was Joseph trying to go to Egypt? No. Was he happy about ending up there? No way.

But God used Joseph's fall from glory to graft him into a bigger plan for *God's* glory.

You see, in the beginning Joseph thought his dreams were all about himself. About his own fame. But as God grew and pruned him through his years of suffering and life circumstances, Joseph realized it was all about something much bigger.

What does our focus verse say God meant Joseph's pain for?

Many years after their separation, Joseph, now a wise financial leader, spoke those words to his brothers in the process of saving them and a swath of the world from a sweeping 7-year famine. He realized that through every trial and every betrayal, God never left his side. He faithfully walked him through his heartache, healed him from his hurt and turned his most searing pain into great purpose. That is our God. His love is faithful, active and healing. He will take your deepest sorrow and transform it into something whole. That's REDEMPTIVE love.

PICK and PRAY

➻ When did you end up somewhere unexpected in your life and how did God meet you there?

➻ What pain would you like to turn over to God so He can redeem and transform it?

➻ What does God's redemptive love look like in your life, and what does it mean to you?

PROCESS

_____

_____

_____

_____

_____

_____

~ Exodus ~

ACTIVE LOVE

And God heard their groaning, and God remembered his covenant with Abraham, with Isaac, and with Jacob.
God saw the people of Israel – and God knew.
Exodus 2:24 - 25

Yesterday we read of Joseph's family moving from Israel to Egypt to escape a widespread famine. The Israelites' story continues in Exodus where we see them now great in number and enslaved by a new king who knows nothing of Joseph or what he did for Egypt. All this new pharaoh sees is a group of foreigners growing too numerous for his comfort. So, in an effort to keep the Israelites from becoming a people so large they might rise up and stage a coup, he puts them under taskmasters and forces them into backbreaking labor. He hopes the back breaking will lead to spirit breaking and a complete breakdown of the Israelite nation.

According to Exodus 1:12, what happened the more the Israelites were oppressed?

Don't you just love that? No matter what may come at God's children, His plan wins out. Every time. That's something for us to remember when life gets twitchy.

You can pick up the story in Exodus 2.

God continues to increase His people, but they remain enslaved. Their heavy burden causes them to "[cry] out for help", and that wail ascends straight into the presence of God. Take a look at your focus verse up top and notice all the ways God responds to that cry.

God hears. God ______________________________. God __________.

God ______________.

Don't you want to know when you call out to God for help He *hears* and *sees* you? He's not sitting idly by while your life threatens to overwhelm you. He is always available and ready to listen. His love for us is attentive, and He's lovingly vigilant.

God also remembers. This is a silly question, but what do you think it means to remember something?

We can't think of this word as we understand it today. It's not as if God forgot the Israelites or the covenant (promise) He had made with them. He's all-knowing after all. The original meaning of this word in the Hebrew is of God being ready to act on something.[1] So, He hears the pleas for help, sees the Israelites' agony and decides the time has come to put His plan of deliverance into motion. God hears the Israelites. He sees them. He knows them, and then He acts on their behalf by sending a man named Moses to lead them to freedom.

If you've accepted Jesus as your Lord, you are just as much God's child as the Israelites were. Just as He saw and heard them, He sees and hears you. Just as He knew them and understood their situation, He knows you – like, really knows you – and understands yours. The best part? He's aware of every single little thing about you and still loves you like crazy – so much that He acts on your behalf when you cry out to Him. Isn't that insane? You are known, and you are adored by a God who listens, sees, and moves out of that compassion for you. That's ACTIVE love.

PICK and PRAY

➤➤ In what situation do you need to actively remind yourself that God's plan will win out?

➤➤ Spend some time thanking God for times when He has delivered you and freed you.

➤➤ What does God's active love look like in your life, and what does it mean to you?

PROCESS

❧ Leviticus ❧
SACRIFICIAL LOVE

This Book of the Law shall not depart from your mouth, but you shall meditate on it day and night, so that you may be careful to do according to all that is written in it.
Joshua 1:8

You may notice our focus verse is from the book of Joshua, and Joshua ain't Leviticus. That's because Leviticus is comprised of 27 chapters completely dedicated to the laying out of the numerous laws of the ancient Israelites. Most times I appreciate God's attention to detail, but here? I struggle, man. Many of my friends feel the same way too. That may be for a couple of reasons. One: Unless you are an attorney or work in law enforcement, reading a list of laws probably ranks low on your Fun Things To Do List. Two: These laws seem irrelevant to us in our New Testament days. The practices outlined on the pages of Leviticus are all about sacrifices and cleansing and Jewish feasts among other things, and we're not really about that life.

However, lately I have found the law can actually be a cool thing, and we benefit a ton from taking a closer look at it. Why do you think it might be beneficial for us to read?

The biggest reason why we in the New Testament church also need to meditate on it day and night, like God tells Joshua, is because it all points to Jesus and our need for Him. Just look!

Most of Leviticus discusses the various kinds of sacrifices that were to be made at the Tabernacle (place of worship). These sacrifices were all about paying for sin and staying in a right relationship with God. For instance, when someone committed an unintentional sin and later realized his guilt, he was to bring an unblemished animal to the Tabernacle, place his hand on the head of the goat or lamb and then kill it. Next, the priest would take a portion of the blood into the Tabernacle to present to the Lord on the altar of incense, returning to then burn the animal on the brazen altar.[2] The blood of the sacrificed animal was meant to cleanse the person from his sin and, thus, clear him and make him right again with God. However, as detailed in Hebrews 10:1-18, it became apparent these sacrifices were never-ending. Because the people continued to sin and the sacrifices and offerings had no permanent or lasting abilities, the priests had to continue to perform them day in and day out. No end in sight.

5

Until Jesus.

> *But our High Priest [Jesus] offered himself to God as a single*
> *sacrifice for sins, good for all time. Then he sat down in the place*
> *of honor at God's right hand . . . And when sins have been forgiven,*
> *there is no need to offer any more sacrifices.*
> *(Hebrews 10:12,18 NLT)*

The unceasing sacrificing exposed our inability to save ourselves and pointed straight to the only One who could – our final sacrifice: Jesus Christ. We have no ability to make ourselves pure or clean, and we sure aren't going to stop sinning completely anytime soon. Thank God for God.

> *For God made Christ, who never sinned, to be the offering for our*
> *sin, so that we could be made right with God through Christ.*
> *(2 Cor. 5:21 NLT)*

We sin and He pays the price. That's SACRIFICIAL love.

PICK and PRAY

➤ What does it mean to you that while you were still sinning Christ died for you (Rom 5:8)?

➤ What would it look like for you to live your life as a thanks offering to Christ?

➤ What does God's sacrificial love look like in your life, and what does it mean to you?

PROCESS

_____

_____

_____

_____

_____

_____

_____

NAVIGATING LOVE

So it was always: the cloud covered it by day and the appearance of fire by night. And whenever the cloud lifted from over the tent, after that the people of Israel set out, and in the place where the cloud settled down, there the people of Israel camped.
Numbers 9:16-17

In Exodus and Numbers, we get a behind the scenes peek at what happened when Moses led the Israelites out of Egyptian slavery. We see all manner of events from miraculous crossings of flood stage waters to a donkey obeying an angel. What I want to take a closer look at today, however, is a pervasive cloud of shade and fire that was camped out in their midst. Go ahead and read *Numbers 9:15-23*.

How do you think the Israelites felt as they set out from Egypt?

I wonder if they felt nervous about what awaited them along their upcoming journey. They were slaves in Egypt, but their days were predictable, and they never had to worry about where their next meal would come from. Do you think they wondered how they would survive on their own with no avenues for income or provision? They were leaving slavery, but they were also leaving the security of the only life they had ever lived. Leaving the known for the unknown.

Have you ever been there – where you left something secure or comfortable with no idea how your leaving would turn out?

It's scary, man. I've done it myself, and the discomfort is almost unbearable if you think about it too much. And I always do. Think and think some more. You too? That overthinking usually leads us straight into what I call a Fear Funnel. We go round and round in our minds and descend into a stopped up, claustrophobic bottle of anxiety. Then we hit the bottom, and we're unable to see a way to unstopper our glass cage and pull ourselves free. All that keeps me from diving into that Fear Funnel in those moments is to depend on God's presence, goodness and direction. That is exactly what the Israelites did in our reading.

The Bible is so cool. Every day of their 40 year journey in the wilderness, God made His presence known to the Israelites by placing a cloud in their midst. That cloud then morphed at night into a pillar that appeared as fire! Isn't that amazing? Not only did the cloud provide shade from the blinding, desert sun during the days, it also provided light and warmth on the cooler nights. I love when God gets practical. It gets even better when we see Him use it to lead them on their desert trek. His clear guidance must have been a comfort in this journey through an unfamiliar land.

We live in a time of unknown too. We may have secure jobs, homes and relationships, but we know our lives could switch direction with a simple nudge from God to go somewhere new. Though He may not send a cloud to do it, God is still in the business of clearly guiding His children, and that is what you are. He has a plan for you, a clear one filled with purpose. As you come to Him, He will reveal that plan and give you everything you need to succeed in it. He is faithful to direct and provide for you. That's NAVIGATING love.

PICK and PRAY

➤ What practical needs can you ask God to provide? Thank Him in advance for meeting them.

➤ Ask God what your next step is with Him, and resolve to trust and obey whatever He says.

➤ What does God's navigating love look like in your life, and what does it mean to you?

PROCESS

_____

_____

_____

_____

_____

_____

_____

_____

_____

❧ Deuteronomy ❧
PERMANENT LOVE

*For you are a people holy to the LORD your God. The LORD your
God has chosen you to be a people for his treasured possession, out
of all the peoples who are on the face of the earth . . . Know
therefore that the LORD your God is God, the faithful God who
keeps covenant and steadfast love with those who love him and keep
his commandments to a thousand generations.*
Deuteronomy 7:6, 9

Being chosen for something is the best. In fourth grade I had a crush on a boy named Troy, and he was so dreamy he could have his pick of any girl in all the elementary world. No joke, I would ask him every single ever-loving day if he would "go with me". This was 1980s speak for *Will you be my boyfriend,* and every day he would politely decline. You would think this would crush a girl's spirit, but no. I just kept asking him, and one day my persistence paid off. He finally said yes! He even agreed to enter the fourth grade jitterbug contest with me. (We took second place.) Aaaah, good times, good times. I look back on those six days with such sweet nostalgia. Yep, six days. That's how long I kept dreamy Troy on my hook. He popped off as quickly as he could get free and swam away to less desperate waters.

Have you ever been temporarily chosen? How did you feel when all was said and done?

It can be a painful experience. Someone has looked at us and found us valuable in some way, and has forever forsaken all others to have us by their side. We are happy and feel special. We've been selected. But then the unthinkable happens, and we are forgotten or downgraded. Maybe abandoned outright. There aren't too many things more painful than this kind of rejection, and if we've ever experienced it, we are at risk for thinking God might do the same.

But God is God; He is not people.

Go ahead and read *Deuteronomy 7:1 - 9*, paying close attention to our focus verses.

Moses tells the Israelites God chose them to be His people, and He treasured them. Treasured. Such a good word. There's nothing quite like being thought that significant. Here's the awesome news for you and me. As soon as we turn our lives over to Jesus, we become children of God. We become His people, and now *we* are His treasured possession!

9

He has chosen *us*!

This is no temporary choice. He never leaves us, never forgets us, and He is a constant help. He's not going anywhere. His choice is permanent. Look at the end of our focus verses: He *keeps* his covenant of steadfast love. His love is a steadfast covenant that he actively nurtures. Whenever we start to doubt God's love, we can look back at the cross and remember He willingly drew up a love covenant and inked it permanent with the blood of His Son. His love for us is not something He takes lightly or dismisses. He paid too much for it. When we accept that payment, we enter into His saving, steadfast love. Forever. He ain't no temporary Troy. He's the real deal, and He's hooked on us eternally. That's PERMANENT love.

PICK and PRAY

➤ Spend some time thanking God for his steadfast, unconditional, never-changing love.

➤ What are you tempted to think disqualifies you from receiving God's love? Surrender that thing and accept God's unconditional, permanent love.

➤ What does God's permanent love look like in your life, and what does it mean to you?

PROCESS

_____

_____

_____

_____

_____

_____

_____

_____

_____

✌ Joshua ✌
TRIUMPHANT LOVE

*And you have seen all that the LORD your God has done to all
these nations for your sake, for it is the LORD your God who has
fought for you.*
Joshua 23:3

Here in our home we are wrapping up our last days of driving our son to school. He will be behind the wheel soon, and we will lose our chance to offer our sagely morning advice. I'm sure he is oh so sad about this development. Though he may roll his eyes now, I know deep down inside his teenaged heart, he loves his dad's parting words every morning: "Be a leader, not a wiener!" Although I'd like to tell Lou to be more appropriate, I can't deny our son has listened to his dad's humorous advice, and we are seeing leadership qualities emerge in his high school years. Maybe Lou knows what he's doing, even if he sometimes does it in a way that makes me wonder if we've cracked our son's moral compass.

Go ahead and read *Joshua 23:1 - 11*.

We see Joshua wrapping up his time of leadership with the Israelites and readying himself to enter into eternity. A mighty warrior, obedient and faithful to do everything the Lord instructed, he had filled Moses's sandals well. As he became aware the sun was setting on his final days, he gathered together the leaders of the community to give them his parting words of guidance.

> *" . . .but you shall cling to the LORD your God just as you have
> done to this day. For the LORD has driven out before you great and
> strong nations. And as for you, no one man has been able to stand
> before you to this day. One man puts to flight a thousand, since it is
> the LORD your God who fights for you, just as he promised you"*
> *(23:8 - 10).*

According to these verses, who was fighting for the Israelites?

We need that reminder too.

Many times in our lives, God will lead us into difficulty. A battle, even. We may not understand His reasons, but just as the Israelites could trust God with their toughest wars, so can we.

Every time God's people followed His direction, no matter how crazy, there was victory. What's stunning is many times it involved God doing something absolutely nutty, like when He had the Israelites march around Jericho, blow their trumpets and shout. God simply made the walls fall down, and His people entered and conquered. What about when He made hailstones fall, and more of the enemy was destroyed by falling ice than by sword? Or how about when He caused the enemy army to turn on itself and destroy each other? It's astounding how far His love will go to protect His people and ensure their victory. He's strong, He's creative and He's on your side.

Our trials may be difficult. Some may even end in heartache here on this side of eternity. But as the children of God, we are guaranteed a win. It may look like peace and joy in the midst of a battle, or it may look like complete deliverance. But one thing is for sure. As we take His hand, God will fight every skirmish for us, and we can rest in His victory. That's TRIUMPHANT love.

PICK and PRAY

➼ What battle are you facing with which God could help you? Express any doubt you may feel, and ask Him to help you believe He will fight for you.

➼ What victories have you seen in your past battles? Ask God to show you and then thank Him.

➼ What does God's triumphant love look like in your life, and what does it mean to you?

PROCESS

*And the LORD turned to him and said, "Go in this might of yours
and save Israel from the hand of Midian; do not I send you?" And
he said to him, "Please Lord, how can I save Israel? Behold, my
clan is the weakest in Manasseh, and I am the least in my father's
house." And the LORD said to him, "But I will be with you"*
Judges 6:14-16a

Man, I love the account of Gideon. You can find it all in Judges 6 - 8, but today,
let's just read *Judges 6:1-34*.

Gideon was an underdog. He was living in a land under constant threat of defeat
and starvation caused by the more powerful people of Midian. These men would
swoop in every harvest season and snatch up the savory new crops and every
single sheep, ox and donkey. Complete devastation. The people of Israel lived in
such fear they built dens, caves and strongholds to hide the fruit of their crops.

Where was Gideon beating out his wheat in 6:11?

This was meant to be done on a hilltop or out in the open so the wind could blow
away the chaff, but here Gideon was in a winepress – a place hidden from any
enemy looking for a free snack.[3]

So we see Gideon not only *was* an underdog, but he thought like one too. His life
was lived simply trying to survive.

Are you there today? Surviving? Have you long given up the dream to do
something more? Have you decided what you've got is all you'll ever have? That
you're never going to conquer that thing that keeps beating you down or stealing
your joy? Read our focus verses and remind yourself what God said to Gideon in
the middle of his hiding and surviving.

Right before this portion of scripture, God called Gideon a mighty man of valor.
I'm thinking Gideon was not feeling very mighty as he hid in a winepress. In fact,
we see that Gideon argued a bit with God's call on his life by listing reasons he
didn't qualify for the call. But God was insistent.

Even though Gideon could not see his worth, God did. And God was intentional in
speaking the truth of who Gideon was directly into Gideon's heart. Not only that,

13

God reassured him that He would be with him every step of the way. That's the real secret of any believer's success.

You are here for a purpose. There is a reason you are alive, and God has a job for you. If you can't believe it, you may have a Gideon complex. And that's okay. We see God's patience with Gideon as he asked God over and over for confirmation of what God asked him to do. He confirmed repeatedly, and one day Gideon got it. He recognized he was indeed who God said he was, accepted His help and then walked powerfully in his calling and saved his people.

God speaks the truth of who you are too, and He does it through His word. You are loved[4], called[5], adopted[6], cherished[7], powerful[8], and wanted[9]. But until we are able to accept those words as truth, we are settling for a hidden, defeated life. You have a powerful calling, and God says you're worthy of it. He created you for it. That's PURPOSEFUL love.

PICK and PRAY

➵ Ask God to show you what He has for you, and then be patient as He answers over time.

➵ What is holding you back from believing God has a call on your life? Surrender it and ask God to strengthen your belief.

➵ What does God's purposeful love look like in your life, and what does it mean to you?

PROCESS

_____

_____

_____

_____

_____

_____

_____

_____

❧ Ruth ❧

ATTENTIVE LOVE

*Where you die I will die, and there will I be buried. May the LORD
do so to me and more also if anything but death parts me from you.*
Ruth 1:17

When teachers discuss the book of Ruth, they often spotlight Boaz and Ruth. Boaz redeeming a destitute Ruth is one of the most beautiful pictures of our redemption through Jesus, and I would recommend you read it if you have the inclination. However, today I want to take a look at an intriguing supporting character: Naomi, Ruth's mother-in-law.

Go ahead and read *Ruth 1*.

My heart breaks for Naomi in this first chapter of Ruth. After fleeing a famine in her home country of Israel with her husband and two grown sons and settling in a foreign land, Naomi loses them all in the span of 10 years. Stop and picture that. The death of her spouse is devastating enough, but losing both of her children too must have just about put her in the grave herself. I imagine her sense of loneliness and abandonment is palpable. Consuming. We can almost reach out and touch her agony when, upon her return to Israel, she tells her family to no longer call her by her given name Naomi but by Mara, a name meaning bitter.

What reason does she give for wanting to be called Mara in verse 21?

Have you ever been in a similar place? One in which you feel if one more thing goes wrong, if you lose one more battle, you're done for? A place you feel almost targeted by God? Yeah, me too. It's an awful place to be. It feels overwhelmingly hopeless.

Maybe it would be without God.

Unbeknownst to Naomi, her widowed daughter-in-law Ruth will turn out to be one of her greatest gifts from God. When Naomi is in her darkest place and engulfed in loneliness, Ruth pledges that she will never leave her. She will go wherever she goes, stay wherever she stays and die wherever she dies. That is fierce loyalty and exactly what Naomi needs. Amazingly, it comes from the most unexpected of places: a young, foreign widow. In that culture, it would have been understood, expected even, for Ruth to leave Naomi and return to her family to either be cared for by her father or to remarry. Yet, she forfeits it all to escort Naomi back to her home country and take care of her as well as she can. What a sweet gift.

God sees us in our most painful circumstances. He is not far off. He is not indifferent. He is not targeting us. He cares deeply. He knows exactly what we need and sends it, sometimes in the most surprising packages. Naomi needs companionship. God also knows she would want a new family, so God sends Ruth, a daughter who refuses to abandon her. I love that the woman who arrives back in Israel wanting to be called Bitter is seen in the final chapter of Ruth surrounded by Ruth and her new husband and child. The curtains close with Naomi holding her new grandbaby Obed, the grandfather of King David and in the family line of Jesus the Christ. She experienced heartbreaking grief, but God sent help to see her through to her heartwarming ending. She is no longer bitter. She can now welcome her true identity, Naomi: "My delight". God gently and systematically nurses her back to emotional health with His thoughtful care. That's ATTENTIVE love.

PICK and PRAY

➤➤ In a dark season? Ask God to open your eyes to the gifts He's sending in the midst of it.

➤➤ Thank God for knowing you and your needs intimately and tending to you intentionally.

➤➤ What does God's attentive love look like in your life, and what does it mean to you?

PROCESS

UNCONDITIONAL LOVE

For as his share is who goes down into the battle, so shall his share
be who stays by the baggage. They shall share alike.
from 1 Samuel 30:24

The account of King David is fascinating. Although he was king, he was also so human that he is relatable to common folk like us. A shepherd boy anointed to replace a rebellious king, David would become one of God's most faithful and powerful servants. But before we get there, let's take a look at David and King Saul's first meeting.

Go ahead and read *1 Samuel 17:13-58*.

Before David even reached the royal court, he was acting more like a ruler than King Saul. The Lord Himself chose Saul for the throne, calling him the prince over his people who would save them from their enemies. Read Saul's reaction to being called to be king in 1 Samuel 9:21 and 10:21-22. What did Saul think about himself and what action did he take because he felt that way?

If only Saul would have believed he was who God said he was maybe his reign would have turned out differently. In contrast, look at 1 Samuel 13:14, where Samuel the prophet speaks to Saul about David, and 17:21-22, where we see David on the battlefield. What did Samuel call David and what action did David take when the Philistines drew up for battle against Israel?

Did you see it? No matter what God said about Saul or what adoration he received from the people, he still thought so lowly of himself that he hid himself among the baggage when God called him. However, David, in spite of being overlooked by his brothers, Goliath and even King Saul, believed God's opinion of him instead. Then he left his baggage where it belonged and busted through it straight into his destiny.

One more little scripture: 1 Samuel 30:21-24.

Much later, David and his men went out to rescue their stolen families from a rampaging army, but many in his army were too exhausted to go with them. Upon returning, many of the fighting men didn't want to share the spoils with those who stayed back. I love David's heart to share everything with them all, because it is a reflection of the way God feels about His children. He is gracious to us all.

No matter who we are, whether we are like David, who leaves the baggage to confidently claim the victory, or like Saul, who hides behind his baggage, or like the group of David's men who become so exhausted that they never even pack baggage to go out, God wants us to know today that we are valuable, cherished, important and loved. We don't have to be good enough, strong enough, ambitious enough, attractive enough, popular enough or successful enough. We all battle. We're all "good" some days and slip up others. That's just part of being human. But God looks at us, no matter what state we're in, and says, "I love you. Period." That's UNCONDITIONAL love.

PICK and PRAY

➼ Do you relate more to David, Saul or the men who remained at home? Why?

➼ Have you had a hard time believing God's love for you? Write a prayer receiving it.

➼ What does God's unconditional love look like in your life, and what does it mean to you?

PROCESS

_____

_____

_____

_____

_____

_____

_____

_____

_____

_____

∂ 2 Samuel ∞

CORRECTIVE LOVE

But the thing that David had done displeased the LORD. And the
LORD sent Nathan to David.
from 2 Samuel 11:27; 12:1

Oh, King David had done it now. When all the kings went out in battle to protect their land or overtake others', David opted to stay home and take a walk on his rooftop. As his men valiantly fought for their king and country, David, safe and cozy in Jerusalem, sauntered high above all and discovered a beautiful woman bathing in a nearby home below.

Go ahead and read *2 Samuel 11:1-17 & 12:1-15* to see the ending to this unsettling beginning.

Maddening, isn't it? David exercised his royal authority to "take" Bathsheba and had what amounted to a one-night-stand that resulted in her pregnancy. What followed next has the makings of 21st century reality television. But this episode ended with an honorable soldier's death and David snatching up his widow for himself.

What part of this account is most disturbing for you? Why so?

Then *the LORD sent Nathan to David.* This is my favorite line of this entire portion of scripture. I look at David's disobedience to the Lord and the resulting deaths it caused, and I shudder to think of the repercussions for David. Honestly, I would not be surprised if God threw in the David towel, turned His back and left David to reap his consequences and dig himself out of his mess alone. But God didn't do that.

The LORD sent Nathan to David.

Nathan the prophet spoke to David, and those words caused him to humble himself and repent. Because of that, God forgave him. Unfathomable. I am taken aback at the willingness of a holy, righteous, just God to forgive such an egregious sin as murder. What kind of love is that? What kind of love looks at something so tragic and premeditated and instead of abandoning, says, "I love you. Give it to me. I forgive you"? Then He allows a repaired relationship to boot. It gives us such hope as we look at all the ways that, despite our good intentions, we sometimes still willingly choose sin over simple obedience. God sees the repentant heart and chooses to forgive and restore closeness with Himself.

19

Unfortunately, although David was pardoned, he still had to face the consequences of his sin. I wish forgiveness were always accompanied by complete removal of any kind of fallout. I hate pain, but what I'm learning about discipline and consequences is they're not mean. They're not vindictive. Just like everything else God does, they are born out of a heart of love for His children. The discipline He lets us endure is for our benefit – to bring us back into emotional intimacy with Him. It's only when we let Him draw us close that He can wrap His arms around us, comfort us, heal us and get us back on our spiritual feet. Even discipline is compassion when handed out by our adoring Father. That's CORRECTIVE love.

PICK and PRAY

➤➤ In what area of your life have you been tempted to believe God to be mean? Ask Him where He was in that area.

➤➤ Is there something of which you need to repent so God can draw you near and heal?

➤➤ What does God's corrective love look like in your life, and what does it mean to you?

PROCESS

৵ 1 Kings ৶

INDIVIDUALIZED LOVE

Now the LORD has fulfilled his promise that he made.
from 1 Kings 8:20

Have you heard of the Enneagram? It's a system to understand the different types of personalities along with their motivations and behaviors. There are nine types. I am a 3 – the Performer – and I have a huge 4 wing. This simply means I have a lot of the traits of a 4, sometimes nicknamed the Individualist. For instance, I tend to reject the norm or trendy. I prefer to be and look distinct. I'm not sure if that's a good or bad thing; it's probably neither. My mom has always called me her little flower child due to my dreamer, hippie ways. I just need room to do me, I guess. I used to be ashamed about this part of myself, and Lord knows when we're growing up schoolmates tease the ones who don't fit in. However, as I've gotten older, I see individuality is exactly what God is after. We see a piece of this in *1 Kings 8:12-23*.

 What did King David want to do but was denied doing by God? Who ended up doing it instead?

This section of 1 Kings details Solomon's actions after he built a temple for God in Jerusalem. Though his father David had wanted to have it constructed, God explained, "You may not build a house for my name, for you are a man of war and have shed blood."[10]

God wasn't condemning David here; the vast majority of the battles David entered into were ordained by God Himself. A huge portion of His purpose for David seemed to be to subdue Israel's enemies through him. Unfortunately, this led to many a day with David covered in the blood of an enemy army, and God didn't want to use those same hands to build His holy temple. I can't fathom war being God's calling upon my life. I would have been fired within the first few hours. Let's everyone just get along and sing camp songs, please.

I wonder if, as a child, Solomon envisioned himself fighting alongside his father. David must have seemed larger than life to a young boy fashioning ideas of how to be a man. I imagine the little tike shadow fighting with a fake sword and shield while bellowing his victory cries. But it seemed God had a different plan for young Solomon.

Solomon's reign was filled with prosperity and peace on all sides. His treasuries were filled to capacity, and people journeyed from far away lands to pay homage to him. Because of his father's work, Solomon's years on the throne couldn't have looked any more different than David's. I'm sure that was quite the relief!

If Solomon would have looked around him and assumed his job was to do what his father had done, he would have built up victories in battle instead of the walls of God's temple. He would have missed his calling, and his ascension to power would have been a waste.

I don't want my life to be a waste.

Find joy today in knowing God's plan for you looks completely different than anyone else's. How reassuring to know God not only loves us enough to give us a purpose, but that He also cares enough to meticulously equip us with everything we need to fulfill that hand-tailored calling. That's INDIVIDUALIZED love.

PICK and PRAY

➻ Ask God what the different thing is He has called you to do.

➻ Who do you need to stop comparing yourself to? What is one way you are fulfilling your individual calling already?

➻ What does God's individual love look like in your life, and what does it mean to you?

PROCESS

☙ 2 Kings ❧
MERCIFUL LOVE

And this occurred because the people of Israel had sinned against the LORD their God, who had brought them up out of the land of Egypt from under the hand of Pharoah king of Egypt, and had feared other gods
2 Kings 17:7

This one gets a bit heavy. It's difficult to skirt around the heavy in 2 Kings, because there is so much evil practiced by the people of Israel and Judah between those pages. By the time chapter 17 rears its head, king after king has reigned and been dethroned. Some rulers practiced God's ways and led in the manner He instructed. However, more chose their own way or their father's way, and this usually included heinous sin and idolatry. That is the environment in which we find ourselves today in this book pulsing with violence and misused power.

Go ahead and read *2 Kings 17:6-24*.

According to verses 6-7, what happened to Israel and why did it happen?

If we read only those two verses and skim the context in which they lay, we might find ourselves thinking God's discipline is too harsh – that it seems drastic for a people who simply sinned just like the rest of us. However, jot down their sinful practices detailed in verses 15-17.

Did you see how they seemed to get progressively worse until they descended to killing their own children as a form of worship to false gods? Doesn't all sin start out that way? Small? We allow our mind to consider something. Then, we think on it more and begin rationalizing it. This causes us to compromise our standards or beliefs a bit, and before we know it, the boundaries we instituted for ourselves have migrated to a completely foreign territory. We look around to find we are so far from God that we have no idea how to get back. Our remedy is to stop ourselves at that first thought and answer it back with truth.

Stop the thought, stop the sin.

Although this portion of scripture is heartbreaking, we see the love of God in verse 13. What did God do through every prophet He sent to His people?

He does the same for us. God sees miles down the long, serpentine road of our lives. He knows what's coming, and when we are about to steer ourselves straight into danger, He warns us to turn back to Him. When we do, we save ourselves from peril we never even saw approaching. He is our heavenly, blinking stoplight. If only the people of Israel would have heeded God's words of caution, they may have saved themselves years of exile and captivity in a foreign land. Though they did not listen and suffered greatly because of it, what they did not endure was a complete wipeout of their people. God could have snuffed them out in one cataclysmic event and started all over, but He chose instead to remove them from their idolatrous comfort zones and replant them in an uncomfortable land. Though He was angry, He did this with the goal of opening their eyes to their need for Him. He did not ruin them. He removed and rescued them from themselves. That's MERCIFUL love.

PICK and PRAY

➤➤ Is there anywhere you are starting to consider compromising your beliefs? Go to God.

➤➤ What warning has God sent you? What were the results of listening or not listening?

➤➤ What does God's merciful love look like in your life, and what does it mean to you?

PROCESS

ᔧ *1 Chronicles* ᔤ

TRUSTWORTHY LOVE

For from day to day men came to David to help him, until there was
a great army, like an army of God.
1 Chronicles 12:22

David's story can get a bit confusing if you're trying to piece it together from the various books of the Bible that tell it. Below is an ordered list of a few of his major life events.

1. David is a shepherd boy
2. He is privately anointed as future king by the prophet Samuel
3. He defeats the giant Goliath
4. He becomes a commander in King Saul's army
5. Saul develops jealousy toward David
6. Saul repeatedly tries to kill David
7. David goes on the run to escape Saul
8. Saul dies
9. David anointed king of Judah, and later, of Israel

There are many other events in his life, but these make up the overall framework to help us put today's account in context. Please read *1 Chronicles 12:1-22; 12:38-40.*

What we are reading today takes place during the time in which David is running from Saul and seeking protection in the surrounding wilderness. He has left his home, best friend, family and life as he knew it. How do you imagine he's feeling at this point?

One of the emotions he is most likely enduring is loneliness. It's traumatic enough to leave everything you know, but to do it alone? Excruciating.

I imagine he is also wondering whom he can trust. We see evidence of that in verse 17 when men come to support David, but he responds with first questioning whether they are for or against him.

They are for him, just as is God.

From an earthly perspective the future looks bleak for David, but we must remember he is the anointed future king. These men are making their way into the wilderness because they believe that promise. Even though Saul's loyal followers can't see it, though Saul chases David down trying to extinguish his impending ascension to the throne, and even as David lives out his days sleeping in the dirt and keeping his head on a swivel, the promise of God still stands. He will, indeed, have David take his rightful place as the king of God's people. He will be known as a God who means what He says.

I wonder, is there a promise God has given you through His word that you need to remember today? If you take your eyes off the chaos around you, what do you need to remind yourself is absolutely true about God? About you? About your future?

Bank on it: no matter what today looks like, God still keeps his tomorrow promises. That's TRUSTWORTHY love.

PICK and PRAY

➤ Remind yourself of one of God's promises to you and that it still stands.

➤ Thank God that His love translates into Him keeping His promises to you.

➤ What does God's trustworthy love look like in your life, and what does it mean to you?

PROCESS

_____

_____

_____

_____

_____

_____

_____

_____

_____

_____

⮡ 2 Chronicles ⮠

HEALING LOVE

For if you return to the LORD, your brothers and your children will find compassion with their captors and return to this land. For the LORD your God is gracious and merciful and will not turn away his face from you, if you return to him.
2 Chronicles 30:9

Second Chronicles is the recounting of the reigns of the kings of Judah (the southern kingdom of God's people). Israel (the northern kingdom) had troubles of its own, but the author of this book empties his ink on the page recording the significant events in Judah's history in particular.

As we begin chapter 29, we are introduced to King Hezekiah of Judah. I hope someday I get to see a playback of him roaring into his reign by immediately and drastically cleaning up the mess his father and predecessor had made. It must have been something to behold. Go ahead and read *2 Chronicles 29 - 30:5* to watch him in action.

Ahaz (Hezekiah's father) had spent his entire tenure on the throne turned away from the Most High God by completely ignoring Him, building altars and sacrificing (sometimes his own children) to idols and nonexistent gods and even cutting some of the temple vessels into pieces and shutting up the doors to God's house. He had no interest in doing things God's way.

According to 29:6-9, what was the result of Ahaz's ungodly leadership?

Sobering, isn't it? God has placed many of us in positions of leadership. Those may be in the workplace, in school, in a ministry or at home. We may even be the person in our circle of friends who tends to call the social shots. What are we doing with that God-given influence? You may be thinking, *I'm not in any leadership role. I don't have any influence.* Yes, you do. If you have any type of relationship at all, you have influence. Let's pray we use ours well.

Thank God for Hezekiah and how he uses his. He sees the ruin brought on by turning away from God and sets instantly to work reestablishing God's place of worship and restoring the service of the house of the Lord. What happens next is the best part of the story. He reinstates the Passover celebration, along with all the other Jewish feasts, that were abandoned by his father. The annual celebration of Passover brings God's people from all over the region to the temple to worship. It is wonderful that God's house is repaired and renewed, but it's what happens because the temple was back in use that is significant. The people come and worship.

God's house has never been about the place. It's about His people.

Look at our focus verse today. Those are the words Hezekiah says to God's children as he tries to convince them to return to the Lord in worship. Those sentiments are for us as well. Some of us are enslaved by captors like anxiety, shame, depression, perfectionism, finances and the like. It's in turning to God in surrender and asking for His help that our freedom is found. That may look a hundred different ways, but it's the turning back that's the key. It's the ceasing of efforts to do it all on our own. We come back to God, and He meets us there to do what Hezekiah did for the sullied temple: clean, restore and reestablish our purpose. That's HEALING love.

PICK and PRAY

➵ What is one action you can take to impact the kingdom with your influence?

➵ What captors would you like to be free from? What is one change you can make in order to turn to God for that freedom?

➵ What does God's healing love look like in your life, and what does it mean to you?

PROCESS

_____

_____

_____

_____

_____

_____

_____

_____

❧ Ezra ❧
DESIGNED & IMPLEMENTED LOVE

And they kept the Feast of Unleavened Bread seven days with joy,
for the LORD had made them joyful and had turned the heart of the
king of Assyria to them, so that he aided them in the work of the
house of God, the God of Israel.
Ezra 6:22

Yesterday we read the account of Hezekiah and his reinstatement of the temple in Jerusalem. We were left with a feeling of hope for the nation as we saw the holy festivals begin anew. However, though his efforts were robust, Hezekiah was only partially effective and his successes fleeting. Unfortunately, the kingdom of Judah fell in 586 B.C. and with it, Jerusalem and the temple. Many of the Judeans were then sent into exile in the foreign land of Babylonia.[11]

After God's people had been in captivity for almost half a century, the Persian king, Cyrus, who was now in power over the defeated Babylonian kingdom, allowed any Jews who desired to help rebuild Jerusalem's temple to return home, and some did.[12] Surprisingly, though, we find in Ezra chapter 4 that they experienced some sneaky opposition and were made to cease all building for a time. That is where we find ourselves today. There is a new king in town (Darius), and the people of Judah have written him a letter requesting he search his records to find that they, indeed, had previously been given permission to build. You can pick up the story in *Ezra 6*. Read through to the end of the chapter to experience the unbelievable movement of God on behalf of His people and His temple.

What is Darius' command to the governor of the province in relation to the building of the Jewish temple, and what is the consequence if that command is broken?

He meant business, didn't he? It gets better. Take a look at 7:6-13 and 7:27-28. Who else went back to Jerusalem?

We now see God's plan opening up before us. His desire to have His temple in Judah rebuilt and for it to be the center of all the reinstated Jewish festivals is moving forward. According to 7:27, how does He accomplish this through His people?

Unbelievable, isn't it? He put it into the mind of a line of foreign kings to allow a group of God's people to leave Babylonia, return to their own country and provide everything they needed from Persian treasuries to rebuild their house of worship and sacrifice to God there. Then the present king went ahead and sent the priests and Levites to perform these duties and any other Judean captives who wanted to go home. Tell me God isn't good!

God is not haphazard. He's not flying by the seat of His holy pants. He has a systematic, good plan for His people in which you play a vital role. He's accomplishing that plan in ways only He could dream up. He leads you tenderly from one well-thought-out step to the next, and He puts everything in place so it's ready to go when you get there. That's DESIGNED & IMPLEMENTED love.

PICK and PRAY

➺ What does it take to design and implement something?

➺ In what area of your life do you need to let God work in a way that is unconventional?

➺ What does God's designed & implemented love look like in your life, and what does it mean to you?

PROCESS

_____

_____

_____

_____

_____

_____

_____

_____

_____

_____

❧ Nehemiah ❧

STRENGTHENING LOVE

For they all wanted to frighten us, thinking, "Their hands will drop
from the work, and it will not be done." But now, O God,
strengthen my hands.
Nehemiah 6:9

Jim Rayburn is one of my heroes. The founder of Young Life was a visionary and soldier for teens in the 1940s when few pastors were considering how to reach them. God dropped a dream for those kids down deep into Jim's soul, and he never let it go. He faced opposition from inside and outside of the ministry, but he was so close to Christ that when he felt God leading him somewhere, he would follow – no matter how crazy those around him believed him to be. There are stories upon stories of Jim accomplishing feats only God could orchestrate. One such instance was obtaining the ministry's first summer camp for an astounding $1 a year! That is a God movement if I've ever heard of one. Because of Jim and others' God-given vision and strength to keep forging ahead, Young Life is now a thriving, international ministry with over two dozen beautiful camping properties worldwide.[13] It's incredible what God can begin with one person.

Yesterday we saw that just as Jim Rayburn set out to accomplish the vision God had given him, Ezra and a group of brave Hebrews ventured out from Babylon to return to Jerusalem and rebuild the temple. Thankfully, they were able to do just that, but the protective wall around the city was still in ruin. It lay as abandoned rubble – a sad reminder of their precious city's degradation. It needed a facelift, but rebuilding that wall was not Ezra's calling. God has something different for each of us to do – our own lanes – and Ezra stayed in his.

Enter Nehemiah.

The king's Jewish cupbearer was devastated when word came that the Jerusalem wall was still in shambles. He quickly arranged a return to Judah to remedy the situation.

God placed a desire (a vision, if you will) on Nehemiah's heart for a repaired wall – one which would be built through his own leadership. He went, but it wasn't always easy.

According to *Nehemiah 4:10-20*, what difficulty did Nehemiah and his men face while trying to rebuild the wall?

31

The opposition came from all directions. The men who sought to stop Nehemiah's work were from the surrounding kingdoms and had their eye on taking ownership of Jerusalem.[14] The threat to Nehemiah's men's lives and their callings was so imminent that they constructed the wall with one hand while holding their weapon in the other. They didn't give up. They refused to stop doing what God had told them to do even though the forces against them were constant.

According to our focus verse, what was it that kept them motivated and able to continue?

God doesn't plant a dream in our heart and then leave it to us to find the wherewithal to make it happen. He doesn't leave us when we face resistance and want to give up. If God has called us to do it, He gives us every ounce of grit we need to get it done. That's STRENGTHENING love.

PICK and PRAY

➤➤ What dream has God placed inside of you?

➤➤ What are different forms of strength needed while following God's call? Ask Him for them.

➤➤ What does God's strengthening love look like in your life, and what does it mean to you?

PROCESS

❧ Esther ❧

STEADFAST LOVE

The Jews had light and gladness and joy and honor. And in every province and in every city, wherever the king's command and his edict reached, there was gladness and joy among the Jews, a feast and a holiday.
Esther 8:16-17

When I was in high school, these magic pictures started showing up everywhere. One day during class change, by friend shoved one of these beautifully patterned drawings in my face. I glanced at it in between discarding my Government book and fetching my Psychology binder. "Pretty."

"No. Look at it. Like, stare at it until you see things start, like, moving." I wondered what she had been smoking. Curiosity forced me to gaze at the blue swirls until my eyes crossed. Just when I was about to chalk up my friend's visions to lack of sleep or something edgier, a 3D shark popped off the surface like he was swimming right there on the page! I tried to reach out and touch him, but I lost my mojo, and everything went flat. Alas, he was hidden within the aqua twirls once more. If I didn't know any better, I would swear there was nothing there, but every time I showed it to someone new, there he would be – hidden in the details. The book of Esther is a lot like those pictures. God is not mentioned one time, but if you search, you will find Him.

Esther was a beautiful, young Jew being raised by her older cousin in a foreign land. One day the king was in need of a new queen, so he gathered all the young virgins to live in his palace. Esther was one of those girls. Here's a quick rundown of her life in the first eight chapters:

1. Esther's parents die and her cousin Mordecai takes her in.
2. The king collects all the young virgins and auditions them in his chambers.
3. Esther finds favor with the eunuch in charge over the women.
4. Esther finds favor with the king and becomes his new queen.
5. Mordecai enrages Haman (the king's vizier) by not bowing to him.
6. Haman convinces the king to order the extermination of all the Jews in retribution. (The king and Haman do not know Esther is Mordecai's cousin and, therefore, a Jew.)
7. Mordecai beseeches Esther to persuade the king to reverse his order.

33

8. Although she knows the king could order her death for approaching him without being summoned, Esther fasts and then asks the king for his ear.
9. Esther reveals the full scope of Haman's plot to kill her and her people to the king.

Read *Esther 7:7 - 8:17* to read the rest of the story.

What happens to Haman, Mordecai and Esther?

The writer of Esther never says anything about God, but we see Him in Mordecai's care of Esther, in the favor she secured from the people in power, in the elimination of her enemy and in the preservation of God's people. Esther, an orphan who surely could have perished alone and forgotten, is instead cared for, given a position of power and used to save a nation. We, like Esther, are not abandoned or outside God's radar. He is right beside us in every season, providing for us, tending to us and using us to impact eternity. That's STEADFAST love.

PICK and PRAY

➤ If you were to make a bullet list of your life, where would you see God?

➤ Do you feel like God is hiding? Ask Him to show Himself to you.

➤ What does God's steadfast love look like in your life, and what does it mean to you?

PROCESS

‍ Job ‍

FEAR-SLAYING LOVE

"Where were you when I laid the foundations of the earth? Tell me,
if you know so much. Who determined its dimensions and stretched
out the surveying line?"
Job 38:4–5 NLT

There ain't nothing like a good humbling. I was pretty pleased with myself my senior year in high school after achieving all my individual and dance team goals. I thought I was unbeatable in all things dance. Periodically, I would catch a glimpse of my mom's mantel display of my awards and think really edifying thoughts about my abilities. I was my own biggest cheerleader.

Then came college.

Though I made it onto the dance team, it became clear I was not God's gift to dance. I got placed left of center in our formations or even – gasp – put in the back! As my goals came up unmet every year, my confidence slumped, and I humbly accepted that I was not created to dance forever.

In the book of Job, our protagonist is deeply entrenched in a level of suffering we could never imagine. He has lost all sources of income, his ten children have been killed, and he has been struck with a painful skin disease. Since he has dedicated his life to walking with God, he is confused as to how God could allow this level of turmoil. He has spent 37 chapters defending his innocence to his friends who believe suffering is a direct result of sin, and now we get to hear God's response in *Job 38:1-20*.

What verse is the most meaningful to you and why?

We see Job's humbling and God's bigness all throughout this chapter – and on into the following chapters as well. If you are a person who doesn't mind folding page corners, I would suggest doing that here. There is truth after truth that we can turn to for reassurance in times when we feel like all hell is breaking loose.

We see God created the earth from nothing. He puts boundaries on the seas, makes the morning appear and sends the darkness scattering. He is even victorious over death. There is absolutely nothing that is outside of His control or power.

If God can create a world of beautifully diverse people and fill them with intricately complex DNA and cells, can He not also devise a creative solution to our most burdensome problems? If He encircles every sea with a confining border, will He not also contain the crashing waves of our suffering so they will not overcome us? If He causes the sun to break the horizon and the moon to usher in the night, won't He also orchestrate the time and length of His purposes and work in our days? Won't He multiply our time when we need it? And if He indeed holds the keys to the gates of death, we don't have to fear it, for we will be escorted straight into His presence when our time here is finished.

God is huge – bigger than we could ever understand – and He has dominion over every facet of our lives. We no longer have to tremble at what may come. As we take His hand, He leads us safely, peacefully and victoriously through it all. That's FEAR-SLAYING love.

PICK and PRAY

➤➤ What feeling do you get when you read how big God is?

➤➤ Surrender your biggest burden to God trusting that He will handle it in the best way for you.

➤➤ What does God's fear-slaying love look like in your life, and what does it mean to you?

PROCESS

✥ Psalms ✥

TENDER LOVE

He restores my soul.
Psalm 23:3a

Psalm 23 is one of the most well-known psalms, so I hesitated to include it in this devotional. I was concerned you might skip right over it due to familiarity. However, to me, none of the other 149 psalms holds a candle to the 23rd psalm in respect to showing God's tender care of His children. So I'm including it. I would encourage you to read the entire psalm before you move on. It's a short one, and I think you'll love it as much as I do.

From beginning to end, we see the attention and care of a strong and vigilant shepherd. He provides everything his sheep need so they are in want of nothing. We see him rid the animal of disturbances so it feels peaceful enough to relax and lay down. He knocks back predators and protects his flock faithfully. But the most captivating sentence is only four words long.

He restores my soul.

We're human, and we will come undone sometimes. Maybe we wander off and create emotional distance between ourselves and God. We may get deeply hurt or so confused that we end up empty or depleted. Possibly we're simply exhausted and need a little refreshment from God. In verse 3, He promises to provide it.

In Phillip Keller's book A Shepherd Looks at Psalm 23, the author compares our downcast souls to a "cast" sheep – a sheep that has rolled over on its back with no ability to right itself. Evidently, this is a common occurrence in the ovine world. If the shepherd does not arrive to roll the sheep over, it is in danger of dying either as a result of the elements or of thirst and starvation. Consequently, one of the shepherd's most important duties is to rise every morning, count his sheep and go out to find the missing, sometimes cast, sheep. And what would Mr. Keller do when he found his sheep? Would he chastise it because it had once again wandered off and gotten itself into this mess? Would he berate it for lying down in a spot that caused the animal to flop over helplessly?

No.

As he carefully righted the helpless animal, massaged its legs to get its circulation moving and steadied it until it could regain its equilibrium, he would "talk to it gently, 'When are you going to learn to stand on your own feet?' – 'I'm so glad I found you in time – you rascal!'"[15]

That is a good shepherd. Can't you just hear the tenderness and fondness? It's no small thing that Jesus is called our Good Shepherd. Just as Mr. Keller searches for his cast sheep and lovingly and gently corrects and restores it, Jesus wraps His arms around us when we are in need of restoration and *gently* loves us back to wholeness. He's not disappointed or shaking His head and rolling His eyes. He's not saying, "I'll help you this time, but you better get it together or else!" He's patrolling the horizon, drawing in any wayward, helpless sheep and speaking restoration sweetly. That is *your* shepherd, and that's TENDER love.

PICK and PRAY

➤ In what area could you ask for God to completely and tenderly restore your soul?

➤ Thank God for any area of your life where you have seen Him restore you and bring wholeness and healing.

➤ What does God's tender love look like in your life, and what does it mean to you?

PROCESS

_____

_____

_____

_____

_____

_____

_____

_____

_____

_____

❧ Proverbs ❧

SAFE LOVE

In the fear of the LORD one has strong confidence,
and his children will have a refuge
Proverbs 14:26

In Houston we don't have basements – unless you count the wine cellars. We just don't need them since we weather hurricanes much more than we will ever endure tornadoes. I have lived in the Houston area most of my life, so I have become hurricane saavy. Tell a native Houstonian there's a tropical storm forming in the Gulf, and we won't even bat an eyelash until our meteorologists tell us it'll be a category 5 hurricane. We've just learned to prepare by stocking up on food, batteries and water, and then we wait until it passes. I thought this is how all storm preparation went.

Then I moved to Dallas.

Y'all. There are tornadoes there. Like, regularly. Did you know you don't get five days notice for a tornado like you do for a hurricane? Life is tootling along, then Boom! There's a crazy whining in the sky – the wail of a tornado siren. The first time I heard it, I wondered if Jesus was announcing His return, and I did a quick scan of the skies as I parked my car. Nobody wants to enter glory in a minivan. Alas, Jesus did not come back that day, but it was the first time I had to run for shelter from a twister. They don't have basements in Dallas either, by the way, and I think, *WHY NOT?? They're a refuge! Why would you not want one?*

Proverbs 14:26 speaks of a refuge of a different sort. It also mentions the fear of the LORD. What do you think that means?

An interesting tidbit about the Bible is it wasn't written in English, so what we read today is a translation of its original language. It's important to understand what the meaning of a verse was when it was first penned. Here, *fear* does not mean to be scared of something. It *can* mean that, but when it's used in the phrase *fear of the Lord* it is more of a respectful reverence.

According to our focus verse, what do we obtain for ourselves and our children when we have this respectful reverence for the Lord?

Though the proverbs are wise sayings more than they are promises, the principles are true. When we revere the Lord, living our lives for Him, we have a confidence in His care of us. If we live that way, it rubs off on the people in our homes and at our jobs and in our schools. It's infectious. When we trust the Lord, people are more aware of His presence. Some of them even start believing simply because they've seen how real and powerful He is in us. Then, when the storms of life roll in, whether we see them coming days before or they appear suddenly, we all know that our God is an impregnable harbor. In the scariest storm, He is a refuge. That's SAFE love.

PICK and PRAY

➤➤ In what area do you need to run to God and let Him be your safe place?

➤➤ Look up Philippians 4:6-7. Peace is another form of refuge. Write that verse below and start doing what it instructs.

➤➤ What does God's safe love look like in your life, and what does it mean to you?

PROCESS

_____

_____

_____

_____

_____

_____

_____

_____

_____

_____

_____

❧ Ecclesiastes ❧

LIFE-GIVING LOVE

"Everything is meaningless," says the Teacher, "completely meaningless!"
Ecclesiastes 1:2 NLT

Sometimes we just need some words of encouragement. Go ahead and read *Ecclesiastes 1:1-11* and prepare to be refreshed!

Lifted your spirits right up, didn't it? I know this seems like a strange part of the book to focus on, but it relays a truth we desperately need to ingest.

If you had to give one phrase or sentence to summarize what you read, what would it be?

I might answer something like, *Life goes on the same year after year, and all of it is meaningless.* You have to wonder what kind of life the author of such sentiments was living. Was he rotting in prison? Steeped in financial debt? At the end of his rope in his love life?

Nope.

He was swimming in riches and wives and considered the wisest man to have ever lived. Solomon – the king of Israel. He had it all, so why would he say everything is meaningless?

We find the answer in 2:24–25. According to Solomon, apart from God we can't find what?

God's presence is the key to finding the joy and fulfillment in our everyday life. I'm thankful God allows us to get to a place sometimes when we see there's *got* to be more to life than what we're living. Otherwise, we may never seek Him out.

 If God's presence is the crux of true life, how do we get into that presence?

- Spend time talking to Him – You can talk to Him like you would talk to your best friend at any time of day. Out loud, silently, in writing, in the shower – whatever!
- Read your Bible – Pick a book and go for it!

- Be still – This one is hard. I have to have a spiral notebook or something to doodle on so I can concentrate on being quiet.
- Go to Church – One that teaches the Bible.
- Start a Gratitude Journal – List things you are thankful God gives you that day.
- Begin a Bedtime Breakdown – Detail the ways in which you saw God that day.
- Go for a walk – Take in all the beautiful things God created.
- Listen to worship music or your local Christian radio station.

You get the idea. You just want to make yourself available to sit in the presence of God and see his perspective. As you do, He will bring eternal meaning into the temporary meaningless. He will bring purpose, joy and fulfillment to your everyday moments. That's LIFE-GIVING love.

PICK and PRAY

➤ What have you mistakenly looked toward to make you happy or bring fulfillment?

➤ What one new practice will you try to implement into your life to begin putting yourself in the presence of God? How often will you do it?

➤ What does God's life-giving love look like in your life, and what does it mean to you?

PROCESS

❧ *Song of Solomon* ❧
COMPANIONATE LOVE

As a lily among brambles,
so is my love among the young women.
Song of Solomon 2:2

Song of Solomon, or Song of Songs as it is sometimes called, is the only book in the Bible I would tag with a PG-13 rating for sensual content. Woo-wee! Hot tamale! Anyone who can read its entirety and still say God isn't interested in marriage being sexually fulfilling is wearing big ol' blinders, in my humble opinion. Side note: this book gives us permission to pray for passion in our marriages when they may be lacking such.

Song of Solomon, ripe with visual nature imagery, details King Solomon's relationship with his beloved wife from courtship to settled marriage. We are privy to their innermost thoughts about their desire for one another and witnesses to one of their misunderstandings and their reconciliation. We might wonder what this is all about. *What is this doing in the Bible,* we might ask ourselves.

Various smart-type people throughout the years have tried to interpret it as symbolic of God's relationship with His people, but there are scads of dissenters on that front. Many scholars don't see any proof or indicators that Solomon was attempting to speak spiritually or metaphorically. He was flat out gushing about how much he adored his wife and she, him. It's a love story, plain and simple. Go ahead and read a beautiful portion of it at *Song of Solomon 1:15 – 2:3*, where you will see the couple speaking ooey gooeys to one another.

Honestly, SOS is not a book I frequent. Affection is not a natural instinct for me, so reading about mushy feelings makes me want to say, "Yeah, yeah. We get it. You love each other. Let's all move on." However, God must have included it for a reason; so, taking pause to search for Him is probably a wise thing to do.

Why do you think God may have wanted this book included as Holy Scripture?

I don't have a definitive answer. Maybe it was to show us what a marriage can look like. Or perhaps it really is a metaphor for His love toward us and we all missed it. We can never be sure, but what we can take away from it today is that God created people for people.

What does God say about man being alone in Genesis 2:18?

God never meant for us to do life alone. We may be single, engaged, married, divorced or widowed. That's not what I'm talking about here. God has different marital plans for everyone. What I am saying is that God gave us mouths so we could speak. He must have wanted us to speak *to* someone. He gave us ears to hear. He must have desired for us to listen *to* one another. We are a gift to each other. We can bear each other's burdens, share in each other's joy and pray for one another. Enjoy each other. God gave us one to the other so we don't have to live lonely. That's COMPANIONATE love.

PICK and PRAY

➤➤ Who has God given you as a traveling companion in this season? Thank Him.

➤➤ In a lonely season? Thank God for His companionship and ask Him to bring you a friend who will be someone with whom you can grow in your faith.

➤➤ What does God's companionate love look like in your life, and what does it mean to you?

PROCESS

_____

_____

_____

_____

_____

_____

_____

_____

_____

_____

❧ Isaiah ❦

FAITHFUL LOVE

"For the mountains may depart and the hills be removed, but my steadfast love shall not depart from you, and my covenant of peace shall not be removed," says the LORD, who has compassion on you.
Isaiah 54:10

What is your very favorite treat in all the world? The one you might not want to even have in your house because you just may down it in one sitting and gain 100 pounds overnight?

Well, around these here parts, there is one cookie everyone in this house knows shall not be touched by anyone but me. Like, don't even glance in its general direction, people. That package of chocolate and cream goodness is all mine. If I swing open the pantry door and reach into the sweets shelf only to return with nothing but out-of-date pasta or a can of misplaced dog food, there will be apocalyptic wails. Fury and fire. Remove my cookies and consider yourself written out of my will. That's all I'm saying. Thank goodness that God is nothing like me in this regard.

Go ahead and read *Isaiah 54*.

Isaiah was a prophet whose purpose in writing was to "display God's glory and holiness through His judgment of sin and His deliverance and blessing of a righteous remnant."[16] He was writing to the people of Judah, but given his language here, we can extrapolate much of what he said to encompass all God's people. This particular chapter speaks of His ancient people's rescue, but when we see in verse 5 that "the Holy One of Israel is your Redeemer", we're left with little doubt who Isaiah is referring to: the coming Messiah Jesus Christ. We know He was not only the Redeemer of Israel, but ours as well. Therefore, we can look at our focus verse and accept its truth for ourselves.

Isaiah paints a picture of hills being removed and mountains being leveled. What word would you would use to describe such a landscape?

It wouldn't look like a simple food item missing from an overstuffed shelf. There would be nothing left but arid spaces and emptiness. It would be a total wasteland. Desolation.

Isaiah 54:10 is an oasis during our arid times. No matter what is taken from us, whether it be a loved one, a job, or something as simple as an opportunity we've been waiting for, God's love for us will not be removed with it. Ever. It will never grow one shade dimmer – even if we are the ones who caused our own pain. We don't have that kind of power. His love remains a constant, vibrant hue through anything you may face and every mistake you may make. When all else fails, God does not.

Not only will God's love for you never change, but He will continue to keep you in this covenantal compassion. Remember your relationship with Him is a promise and not contingent on your good behavior. He is steadfast. He will not reject you, and His actionable love is something you can depend on every day – even if you steal someone's cookies. That's FAITHFUL love.

PICK and PRAY

➻ Spend time thanking God for continuing to love you and keep you through all your mistakes and disobedience.

➻ In what part of your life do you need to remember that God's love for you will not or did not lessen?

➻ What does God's faithful love look like in your life, and what does it mean to you?

PROCESS

_____

_____

_____

_____

_____

_____

_____

_____

❧ Jeremiah ❧

SUSTAINING LOVE

*"Blessed is the man who trusts in the LORD, whose trust is the
LORD."*
Jeremiah 17:7

As we continue on with the prophets of the Old Testament, it's important to know the purpose and historical context of these brave messengers. They were sent out to Israel and Judah as a warning of impending judgment or as comfort when judgment had been enacted. Both countries were eventually captured and put into submission to enemy armies because of their continued, defiant disobedience to the Lord. No matter how many messages of caution He sent through these faithful prophets, the people wouldn't listen and ended up in captivity.

Jeremiah had one of the toughest gigs of all of the prophets. Though all God's heralds delivered unwelcome messages at some point, Jeremiah isn't called The Weeping Prophet for nothing. His entire 40-year ministry consisted of warning the people of Judah that if they didn't turn away from their idols and false gods and turn back to God, they would face judgment. And for four decades, they ignored him. He shed many tears over his unrepentant countrymen.

However, in chapter 17, the somber tone is broken with some beautiful news. Go ahead and read *Jeremiah 17:5 - 8*.

What does God call the man who trusts Him in verse 7?

Smack dab in the middle of this book announcing curses, we find how we can be truly blessed. We must trust the Lord. What do you think it means to trust someone?

Trusting, in this context, means exactly what we think it means: to put our confidence in something. Usually when we do that, action comes next. For instance, if we put our confidence in a chair's ability to hold us, we'll sit down in it. Trust is a foundational piece of our relationship with Christ. If we are going to move forward in His purposes for us, we have to believe what He says is true and that He is good.

When we practice putting our confidence in Jesus, a wonderful result blooms. Like a tree abiding by a nourishing river, our life begins to produce fruit.

According to Galatians 5:22, what nine qualities make up the Fruit of the Spirit?

As we plant ourselves in the continual presence of God and trust Him unwaveringly, the Holy Spirit goes to work on us. Before we know it, our roots are drenched in the Living Water, and we notice a higher level of joy. People don't get under our skin as much as they used to. And if we find ourselves surrounded by a sweltering drought of the soul, we have more peace than seems normal. That is the power of Christ. Through even the driest seasons, we can trust He is near, nourishing and nurturing us to vibrant life. That's SUSTAINING love.

PICK and PRAY

➤➤ How is your trust level with Jesus? In order to trust Him more, write down times in the past when He has come through for you or sustained you.

➤➤ What message has God been giving you? Choose to trust it.

➤➤ What does God's sustaining love look like in your life, and what does it mean to you?

PROCESS

_____

_____

_____

_____

_____

_____

_____

_____

_____

_____

❧ Lamentations ❧

UNDETERRED LOVE

The steadfast love of the LORD never ceases;
His mercies never come to an end
Lamentations 3:22

Have you ever been listening to a sermon or reading the Bible and a word or phrase jumps up and slaps you silly? You know from what you've just heard or read that you need to attend to this area of your life, like, pronto quicko? I had that moment a few of weeks ago when my pastor said, "Some of us need to turn our whining into worship."[17] Oof. His point was that what we focus on is important. I thought, *Misti, from now on, when you feel like whining, make the choice to find something to worship God for.*

We get to see a bit of that today in *Lamentations 3:19 - 24*. Go ahead and give it a read.

The author of Lamentations isn't whining; he is mourning, and mourning is important. It's important that we feel our feelings. The majority of what he writes is lamenting the destruction of Jerusalem, but he changes his focus in chapter three.

According to 3:22-23, what lasts forever, and what is new every morning?

That reminder never gets old. When we feel like we've blown it or done something we think might make God turn up His nose at us, we are comforted by the truth that there's nothing we can do to stop His love. It's ongoing. When we open our eyes to new light every morning, He opens up His hands filled with new mercies. A fresh start. Every single day. Praise your name, God!

In the midst of his mourning, the writer also reminds himself that God's faithfulness to His people is "great". That word seems to lose its effectiveness in our culture since we can describe a piece of pizza as great and then turn around and use that same word to describe a person: "She is so great!"

In the original language, *great* has the feeling of more than enough. An abundance.[18] If we put that in context, God's faithfulness toward us is *more* than enough. In whatever way we need to have Him come through in our lives, He's got more.

In fact, if you read 3:22-24, there is an overall sense of God running over with love, mercy and faithfulness for us. The enemy tries to get us to believe that God is mad at us or disappointed with us. But the truth of God's character is written right here in this book of mourning: He loves you now; He will continue to love you, and He is faithful and merciful every day of your life.

This is what my pastor spoke into my heart that day a few weeks ago. No matter what state we're in, whether we are grieving, in a season of celebration, or somewhere in between, the key to our joy in the Lord is where we choose to focus.

When we rejoice, are we giving God the glory? When we mourn, are we finding our footing in Jesus? You'll notice in verse 24, the lamenting author finds his joy in focusing on God's character. We will too when we remember that He is ever loving, merciful and faithful. That's UNDETERRED love.

PICK and PRAY

➤➤ What new mercy do you need today? Ask God for it.

➤➤ Thank God that there's nothing you can do to separate you from His love.[19]

➤➤ What does God's undeterred love look like in your life, and what does it mean to you?

PROCESS

_____

_____

_____

_____

_____

_____

_____

_____

❧ Ezekiel ❧
FORGIVING LOVE

*"Say to them, As I live, declares the Lord GOD, I have no pleasure
in the death of the wicked, but that the wicked turn from his way
and live; turn back, turn back from your evil ways, for why will you
die, O house of Israel?"*
Ezekiel 33:11

One of my favorite events in any routine day is the curt ring of our doorbell announcing a package has been dropped on our doorstep. It's even better if I don't know it's coming. The UPS workers have one of the best jobs in the world. Imagine – their entire trade consists of delivering joy wrapped in Amazon packaging all day long. If they have the time to, they can wait and watch a person open her door, bend down to retrieve her parcel and then smile ear-to-ear. They made that happen. Their task is to deliver happiness!

Ezekiel delivered too, but what he had to give didn't bring much pleasure. Go ahead and read *Ezekiel 33:1-11*.

What does God call Ezekiel in 33:7?

Son of man simply means that Ezekiel is human, but God also calls him a watchman. Did you catch how significant his role was? God was conveying words of warning for Ezekiel to pass on to Judah, and if he didn't, their judgment would fall on Ezekiel as well. Yikes. Not as fun as Amazon.

Zeke has spent most of the book warning of God's impending judgment on His people who have forfeited their faith. Chapter after chapter outlines the sin of Judah and her surrounding nations. God warns and warns and warns some more. It seems so dark and hopeless.

But then comes 33:11. What does God say about Himself?

We may read the Old Testament and conclude that God must get some kind of sick satisfaction from seeing the destruction of people pitted against Him. Honestly, many of us take a metaphorical sigh of relief when we finally see Israel's tormenters get what they seem to deserve. How could we not?

But God is not like us.

51

There are no positive vibes surrounding Him when the wicked get their dues. He does not wait on the edge of His throne anticipating the time He finally gets to push the red button. He is saddened.

He wants even the most evil to turn back to Him and live.

Truth be told, we are much like ancient Judah sometimes. We choose to bow down to our own idols: comfort, technology, family, success, control – anything we turn to instead of God or prioritize above Him.

What is one thing you tend to turn to instead of turning to God?

God is not excitedly anticipating the day He must punish you for that idolatry. He's whispering, "Turn from that and live. I have more for you." That's FORGIVING love.

PICK and PRAY

➤ What is that one thing for which you need to accept forgiveness? Leave it here.

➤ Thank God for His forgiving heart and His complete forgiveness.

➤ What does God's forgiving love look like in your life, and what does it mean to you?

PROCESS

❧ Daniel ↩

GREAT LOVE

*As for these four youths, God gave them learning and skill in all
literature and wisdom, and Daniel had understanding in all visions
and dreams.*
Daniel 1:17

Hey, welcome back! Let's start today by diving right into our scripture portion. Go ahead and read *Daniel 1*.

You may have heard of Daniel and the Lion's Den or Daniel with his buddies Shadrach, Meshach, and Abednego; this is that same man. We read that this is the point in Israel's history when he and a host of others have been taken into Babylonian captivity. How would you describe the Daniel of chapter one?

He's pretty great, isn't he? Good looks aside, he is a young man (many scholars think a teen) of integrity and whole-hearted devotion to God. Despite that dedication, he enters into what is probably the scariest time of his life to date. He is seized and put under the authority of Babylonian educators and eunuchs. Though he is given rich food from the king's table, Daniel and his buddies resolve to remain clean in God's sight by abstaining from that food. From his conversation with the chief eunuch, we learn this decision could be deadly for all involved. However, according to 1:9, what did God do to ensure Daniel could honor his devotion to Him?

In his captivity, God was moving. Israel may have been defeated, but Daniel was not.

We may be down, but God makes sure we are not out.

God uses this time of defeat for a bigger purpose and equips the boys with everything they need to walk in that purpose: learning, skill, wisdom and for Daniel, the ability to interpret visions and dreams. Not only do they have everything they need to flourish, the king finds them ten times better than his best wise men.

When we cooperate with God, He gives us more than enough for the season we're in.

As the book of Daniel continues and Daniel's time in Babylon ticks away, a couple of the kings have disruptive dreams, and Daniel is called upon to translate them. He walks straight into the royal court and proclaims that God Almighty is the only One who could ever decipher the meaning of these dreams. He then gives accurate interpretations of them, and the kings briefly acknowledge the one true God. They see Him. They hear the Truth. They know the Truth. They have been told.

All because one man lived that Truth boldly. Every day.

Daniel later goes on to give detailed, vivid prophecies that we are still waiting to be completely fulfilled. What he learned in his darkest times, God used to enlighten us all.

According to 9:23, why does God speak to Daniel?

God calls him "greatly loved" twice more in chapter ten. God communicates to Daniel out of an immense love for him. His love for His people is so considerable it moves Him to interact and equip us. It prods Him to action on our behalf and for His glory. That's GREAT love.

PICK and PRAY

➵ Where else can we see God's great love in the Bible?

➵ Thank God that His great love causes Him to act on your behalf.

➵ What does God's great love look like in your life, and what does it mean to you?

PROCESS

_____

_____

_____

_____

_____

_____

_____

_____

❧ *Hosea* ❧

PARENTAL LOVE

When Israel was a child, I loved him, and out of Egypt I called my son.
Hosea 11:1

I mentioned a few chapters back that I'm of the opinion that Jeremiah had one of the most difficult prophetical callings in the Old Testament. There's only one prophet that has him beat in ministry misery: Hosea.

What does God instruct Hosea to do in 1:2?

Hosea not only had to deliver the message of God's displeasure with Israel's unfaithfulness, his life became a living illustration of that message. Can you imagine choosing to marry someone you knew would break your heart by turning to another? Honestly, I don't know if I could willingly subject myself to that trauma. I guess that's why Hosea was a prophet and I'm not. He obeyed. Please read a bit more of his story in *Hosea 11:1-8*.

Hosea's wife Gomer played the adulteress just like God said she would, and Hosea ended up having to buy her back from another man she had gotten herself entrenched with. Hosea had to fork out his own hard-earned cash to redeem a woman who had no interest in being his wife.

How do you imagine he felt upon that transaction? Picture it in detail.

We don't know all the details such as how Gomer felt in all of this, but I can only assume Hosea was humiliated.

Do you see the resemblance in Gomer and Israel? Just as she had turned away from Hosea to enter another man's house, Israel had rejected God to worship idols. God's love runs deeper than a marital relationship, however.

What does God call Israel in 11:1?

Israel's relationship to God will always be that of son to Father. In 11:3, we can picture a daddy grasping his little one's plump hands and holding her up as she tentatively takes her first steps. In 11:4, He is leading with kindness and love. He yearns to ease their burden. In 11:8-9, we feel His anguish as He considers the discipline He must administer.

55

This is the heart of a loving Father towards His beloved, disobedient child.

What does 2 Corinthians 6:18 call God's people?

If you have begun a relationship with God, you are now His child as well! Go back and read 11:3-4 thinking of yourself as the recipient of God's actions found there.

Even before you knew God, He was working behind the scenes. He took your hand and taught you how to walk – spiritually and emotionally. He continues to lead you with cords of kindness and bands of love. When we spit in the face of that love and He is forced to discipline us, it tears Him up. He is the fully-invested Father who loves wholly, humbly, actively, and selflessly. That's PARENTAL love.

PICK and PRAY

➤➤ What has God done for you that you didn't even realize He was doing until later? Thank Him.

➤➤ How is God leading you now with cords of kindness and bands of love? Follow Him.

➤➤What does God's parental love look like in your life, and what does it mean to you?

PROCESS

_____

_____

_____

_____

_____

_____

_____

_____

_____

❧ Joel ❧

PROVIDING LOVE

Even the beasts of the field pant for you because the water brooks
are dried up, and fire has devoured the pastures of the wilderness.
Joel 1:20

As we move through the prophets, the messages of doom can get pretty wearying. I don't know about you, but if I've had a bad day, I'm not rushing over to my Bible and flipping to locate the book of Jeremiah. However, my hope in these 66 days is that even in the most difficult of messages, in the darkest days of God's people, we still find God's love. He never changes. He didn't one day decide He was going to start being more compassionate. The same Love that caused Him to rescue us on the cross bleeds on the pages of the Old Testament. We may just have to look a little harder to unveil it.

Go ahead and read *Joel 1:13-20*.

If I absolutely demanded that you tell me where you might see a glimpse of God's love in those verses, what would you say?

I wish I could hear your answers. Some of you might have seen God's love in His sending a warning. He could easily squash the disobedient without any kind of tip-off at all, but He chooses not to. Maybe you said the fact that He cares enough to discipline shows He loves us.[20] Possibly you noted that His willingness to accept our repentance demonstrates His devotion.

All those are valid and comforting. Take another look at verses 19-20. To whom do Joel and the beasts of the field cry out?

Why would they cry out to Him?

In their desperate need, God is the One who can do something about it.

Write Psalm 147:8-9 below.

Take a look out your window and drink in nature. God caused all that. Trees and grass didn't just pop up out of the ground on their own. I know it seems that way, but God purposed and placed them through the natural processes of growth He designed. From the lavender lilacs beautiful to the banana tree ripe, none of it is an accident.

What does Philippians 4:19 say God will provide?

He doesn't only give natural provisions. Every need you could ever have – physical, emotional, spiritual – God promises to supply. He doesn't miss a thing. He sees every area of lack and is attending to it. That's PROVIDING love.

PICK and PRAY

➼ Surrender any needs to God and ask Him to help you release any desires He does not want for you. Trust Him – there's a reason He won't give it to you. Remember He's good.

➼ Thank God for any way He has provided for you lately.

➼ What does God's providing love look like in your life, and what does it mean to you?

PROCESS

_____

_____

_____

_____

_____

_____

_____

_____

_____

❧ Amos ❧

LONG-SUFFERING LOVE

*"I struck you with the blight and mildew; your many gardens and
your vineyards, your fig trees and your olive trees the locust
devoured; yet you did not return to me," declares the LORD.*
Amos 4:9

Ever so briefly, let's consider an important subject most of us tend to ignore because we simply don't like thinking about it much: our need to forgive. Wait! Don't skip this one – I won't make you think about it for more than these two paragraphs. I promise. Take a quick jog over to the New Testament and find Matthew 18:21-22. How many times does Jesus tell Peter we need to forgive someone?

That doesn't actually mean 490 times. Unfortunately, we're not off the hook when Snarky Sara throws a verbal punch for the 491st time. What Jesus meant was that our forgiveness should be never-ending. We've gotta do it every single stinkin' time. I don't mind saying this is one of my least favorite teachings of Jesus'. I'm award-winning at holding a grudge.

This level of pardoning may seem like a feat we simply can't accomplish, but God isn't asking us to do anything He's not doing Himself. Take a look at *Amos 4:6-13*.

What does the Lord declare at the end of every section?

We know these prophets were in the business of warning God's people, but we see here in Amos they weren't the only avenues God used to do so. As God sees the Israelites continue in their rebellion, in their sins against Him, He goes about calling them back.

How does He do so?

We can't jump to the conclusion that all bad circumstances are a result of sin. That's not biblical. As we witnessed in Job, sometimes, through no fault of our own, this fallen world simply falls on us. We can be thankful God sees us in those times and upholds and heals us through them. However, we can't deny there are times when God is trying to get our attention.

Will we listen?

Thankfully, if we walk away from God, He sends a warning. And then He'll send another one. Heck, in our scripture today alone, He sent messages through lack of food and rain, along with pervasive mildew and more. He kept sounding the alarm even when no one responded.

This is the God with whom you have a relationship – the God who gives us caution after caution. The God who has grace after grace after grace. He doesn't just uncaringly glance our way when we start to wander off or just write us off and forget us. He wants us to live with Him so badly that He keeps calling us back until the day we perish. That's LONG-SUFFERING love.

PICK and PRAY

➤➤ Has God given you a warning lately? What did it look like? What is your response?

➤➤ Write out a prayer like the following: God, I know you love me and want to do life with me. When I start to move away from you, please help me hear your warning and come back. I know that's the only place I will find real peace and joy.

➤➤ What does God's long-suffering love look like in your life, and what does it mean to you?

PROCESS

_____

_____

_____

_____

_____

_____

_____

_____

_____

❧ *Obadiah* ❧

CONQUERING LOVE

But in Mount Zion there shall be those who escape, and it shall be holy, and the house of Jacob shall possess their own possessions.
Obadiah 1:17

I have the cutest little Schnese you ever did see. You may feel the need to bless me with a hearty "Gesundheit", but there is no need. A Schnese is a dog – a Miniature Schnauzer and Havanese hybrid – and our Finn may be the most entertaining one ever bred. Although his lofty Havanese ideals insist we serve him in a manner pleasing to his royal Cuban ancestors, his Mini Schnauzer instinct takes over as soon as he spies a squirrel. All decorum is lost as he sheds his fancy pants and bolts out the door like the ratter he was bred to be. Poor thing. No matter how fast, he never satisfies his critter craving. The chase always ends the same: squirrel atop our fence gazing down his pretentious little nose as if to say, "Ha! Like you could catch me, frou-frou dog with your silky, black hair and perky ears." I fear Finn is destined for defeat forever.

Go ahead and read *Obadiah 1*. Key terms: Obadiah – the prophet speaking, Edom/Esau – enemy country of God's people, Judah/Jacob/Jerusalem/Joseph – God's people.

Edom and God's people had been at odds since the days of Jacob and Esau. There are numerous references to Edom and her transgressions against Israel in the Old Testament. So, it's no surprise when we read that God has seen her violence and is planning her destruction. In the chart below, note the words used to describe what happened to Judah and Edom's reactions to it in 1:10-14.

Judah   Edom

Judah's defeats were overwhelming. As we hear her described with words like *ruin* and *disaster,* we might wonder if she will ever find any kind of victory at all. What do verses 17 and 19-20 say will become of these people?

When Jesus comes back to reign on this earth, there will be no more crushing for Israel. She will be united, will inherit her land once more and Jesus will reign over her as the King of Kings. Praise the Lord!

As God's children we are never meant to live in defeat. God calls us more than conquerors through Christ who loved us[21] and tells us we have the power to demolish strongholds[22] in our lives. We don't have to live small, deflated, overcome lives. Jesus died on that cross so we could know Him, believe Him and walk in His freedom and power. If we choose to believe and obey Him, He will ensure our victory. That's CONQUERING love.

PICK and PRAY

➤➤ Confess any time you have rejoiced over someone's downfall like Edom.

➤➤ In what area are you feeling defeated? Look up a scripture that is the truth for that area, write it below and pray it over your life.

➤➤ What does God's conquering love look like in your life, and what does it mean to you?

PROCESS

❧ Jonah ❧
COMPASSIONATE LOVE

"for I knew that you are a gracious God and merciful, slow to anger and abounding in steadfast love, and relenting from disaster."
from Jonah 4:2

Normally I ask you to read a small portion of scripture, but today I am asking a little more of you. I hope you don't mind. I'd like you to read all four chapters of Jonah: *Jonah 1-4*. That may sound like a lot, but in my Bible it is only 2 ½ pages, so I hope you'll indulge me. I will be pulling from all chapters, so it will help you pick up what I'm laying down if you've read the entire story. It's a good one. You'll enjoy it, so go ahead on, then, and read this crazy account of a man and his fish.

If you grew up in the church or have had any type of exposure at all to the Old Testament, you've probably heard about Jonah.

What is one new thing you learned today about Jonah's story?

We tend to think about Jonah's disobedience and the big fish and leave the rest in the background. Or, at least I do. When we do this, we miss all the other players and how God showed off for them. We also focus on Jonah's disobedience and get tempted to see the big fish as punishment. However, if we pan out, take the story as a whole and look at all the people involved, God's compassion takes center stage.

The Shipmates – The victims. We feel for the other travelers on the boat, don't we? They have been hurled into the center of someone else's storm and are paying for another's rebellion. It just doesn't seem fair. Maybe it isn't, but here's the awesome thing. God saves them too. He hears their cries, and when they listen to the instructions of Jonah, the man of God, all goes quiet. They are rescued.

Jonah – The rebel. It's interesting to consider this man of God was also a bit of a maverick. That gives me some comfort since I also have a little of that Don't-Tell-Me-What-To-Do spirit. When the fish approaches and swallows up Jonah, I want us to see his reaction.

"The waters closed in over me to take my life; the deep surrounded me . . . yet you brought up my life from the pit, O LORD my God." (from 2:5-6)

63

This fish wasn't punishment; the fish was deliverance. Jonah knew he deserved whatever he received for turning his back on God, but God sent rescue wrapped in scales and fins instead.

The People of Nineveh – The despised and loved. After being vomited up on the shore, Jonah decided he would, indeed, obey God and warn the Ninevites of God's displeasure with their evil practices. We see in chapter four he did it unwillingly, his palpable disgust for the people still choking out his joy. But whom Jonah hated, God loved enough to send warning of impending judgment. Oh, I pray we the church, the people of God, would love with word and action those whom the world despises.

We see the manifestation of our focus verse vibrantly showcased in every person's experience in the book of Jonah. We can thank God that whether we are in the wake of someone's rebellion or are the rebel ourselves, God is slow to anger, abounding in love and quick to relent from disaster. He does not long for our punishment; He delights in sending deliverance. That's COMPASSIONATE love.

PICK and PRAY

➤ Which people in this account do you relate to the most? Why? Where is God in your story?

➤ Who in your life could use some mercy and compassion? Could you be the one God uses to show that?

➤ What does God's compassionate love look like in your life, and what does it mean to you?

PROCESS

_____

_____

_____

_____

_____

_____

✺ Micah ✺
PREPARATORY LOVE

*But you, O Bethlehem Ephrathah, who are too little to be among
the clans of Judah, from you shall come forth for me one who is to
be ruler in Israel, whose coming forth is from of old,
from ancient days.*
Micah 5:2

Have you ever gone to the store to find something, but you weren't quite sure what you were looking for? Girls, how many times have you gone shopping for a party or a wedding, and didn't know exactly what you were looking for – you just knew nothing in your closet would make the cut? It's frustrating because you have no clear direction. If the invitation said, *wear a mid-length dress with heels and statement jewelry*, we'd be good to go. But no directives leave us meandering about wondering what it is we're searching for.

We can be thankful God isn't into meandering or confusion. Go ahead and read <u>Micah 5:1-5</u> to see what I mean.

Micah was another prophet announcing coming judgment for great sin. However, we can be grateful because he is not all gloom and doom. Messages of hope weave themselves throughout his chapters, particularly as we read about the future restoration of this disobedient nation.

Some of that hope comes in 5:2. Who does Micah say will come forth from Bethlehem?

Who do you think that will be, specifically?

If you gave the church answer (Jesus), you are correct! Ding Ding! There will be a ruler who will come to shepherd His people in strength and majesty. Here's a cool thing: Micah uttered these words 700-800 years before Jesus was even born![23] How awesome is God?

There are other places that tell of the coming King. What do the following verses say about Him?

Isaiah 7:14 –

Zechariah 9:9 –

Jeremiah 23:5 –

Isaiah 53:3-6 –

Psalm 22:14-18 –

These were all written hundreds of years before Jesus' birth, and there are tons more. Our eternity is determined by whether or not we know Christ, so how caring of God to make sure we knew exactly who He was when He showed up. He gave us clear direction so we would know how to respond. God ensured we had everything we needed to keep us from missing the Messiah. That's PREPARATORY love.

PICK and PRAY

➥ Which prophecy is the most interesting to you? Why?

➥ Thank God for making your eternity easy to find.

➥ What does God's preparatory love look like in your life, and what does it mean to you?

PROCESS

_____

_____

_____

_____

_____

_____

_____

❧ *Nahum* ❧
REFUGE LOVE

The LORD is good, a stronghold in the day of trouble;
he knows those who take refuge in him.
from Nahum 1:7

Nahum does not play. I can't imagine being a prophet walking into a city to deliver the news that the Lord is going to bring complete ruin. No thank you very much. My people pleasing tendencies would throw a hissy fit to rival the most entitled celebrity. If we were to read all three chapters of this small but powerful book, we would hear Nahum line out the destruction of the Assyrian capital city of Nineveh. They had oppressed God's people, and their time of payment had arrived. It's a tough book to read, but it reminds us that God is fiercely protective of His people.

Go ahead and read *Nahum 1:2 - 7*, please.

How would you describe God after reading this?

Although God is depicted as enraged at His enemies and in the act of taking vengeance on them, we also get a glimpse of His incredible power. His ways are described as torrential weather conditions, and we see how easily He controls the sky, sea and land. Even the majestic mountains shiver in His shadow.

Fill in verse 7:

The LORD is _____ , a _____

in the day of trouble; he _____ those who take refuge in him.

(ESV)

If we don't stop and take notice of this verse right here, we are liable to get overcome by God's power and miss His benevolence. Inundated with God's wrath in this book, we benefit from hitting pause to look at the three words we filled in. They are refreshment in the desert of Nineveh's judgment.

Good – We see God's power everyday through His creation and sustaining. Isn't it awe-inspiring to know that same God – the One who can push up Mt. Kilimanjaro from flat ground – is also sweet and *for* you? He's not only immensely powerful, He's good. If we have one without the other, our view of God is left wanting. He is fully powerful and fully good.

A stronghold – He is an impenetrable fortress for us when life becomes a battering ram. That strength and goodness He wields leads Him to actively envelop and protect the ones He loves when we are attacked from all sides.

He knows us. – *Knows* is translated different ways depending on which Bible version you're reading. Circle your favorite: *knows, is close to, cares, recognizes and welcomes, understands fully.*

This is the kind of God we get to serve! He is not only strong, but He knows who we are, welcomes us, understands us fully, and draws us close in protection. That's REFUGE love.

PICK and PRAY

➤ Which bolded description of God from 1:7 impacts you most? Why?

➤ Why did you choose the word you circled? Talk to God about that.

➤ What does God's refuge love look like in your life, and what does it mean to you?

PROCESS

_____

_____

_____

_____

_____

_____

_____

_____

_____

_____

◌ Habakkuk ◌

RELATIONAL LOVE

*GOD, the Lord, is my strength; he makes my feet like the deer's; he
makes me tread on my high places.*
Habakkuk 3:19

Have you ever been relaying the hilarity or difficulty of your day to someone and then realized your friend's eyes are as glazed over as a jelly donut? Nothing gets me quite as wound up as starting a conversation and losing my one-person audience. *Like, am I not entertaining enough for you? How about if I put on this funny hat and make a fart noise? Will that keep you from spending time with the person inside your smart watch instead of this enchanting person sitting right across the table?* I have soapboxes, and this is one of them.

Habakkuk opens with the prophet already knee-deep in his own conversation. Amazingly, it is with God Himself – the most attentive audience. As he laments how God can allow the horrific violence and sin he sees around him in Judah, we wonder what type of response he's going to get from the Lord of Lords, who isn't obligated to explain Himself to anyone. God created Habakkuk and is perfectly within His rights to handle his inquiries however He sees fit – or not handle them at all. It's in these moments, when imperfect people approach our perfect God with questions I myself have, that I turn up my ears. I need to know too. Why, God? Why does evil sometimes seem to go unpunished?

What is God's answer to Habakkuk's question according to 1:5-6?

That's probably not the answer he was looking for. Pain is not always caused by sin, but here we see it is. God is raising up an enemy army to invade Judah and take her captive as a form of discipline. This, of course, confuses Hab, and he and God continue to converse through all of chapters two and three. According to 2:3, what is awaiting its appointed time?

That vision is one in which the invading army will face divine judgment for conquering God's people in Judah and carrying away her inhabitants. Babylon's actions may be allowed as an instrument of correction for Judah, but God does not let her evil go unpunished. He is entirely loving, but He is also just. Babylon as a whole, unfortunately, was characterized as a nation who had turned her back on God completely, and was thus, subject to His wrath.

69

I'm grateful for the knowledge that God sees it all – all the injustices and pain and hurt perpetrated by others. We can rest in knowing He's dealing with them out of his loving and just nature in His own time – the perfect time.

As reassuring as that truth is, what is more unbelievable is that God even enters into conversation with Habakkuk at all. Get this: He does the same with us. When your God loves you enough to lean in as you pray, it instills the same confidence this faithful man displays in *Habakkuk 3:17-19*. Though there will be discipline, though we sometimes must suffer, we know that our God loves us so deeply that He will steady our feet to navigate the rough terrain and see us all the way through to our spiritual victories. He enters in. Every time. That's RELATIONAL love.

PICK and PRAY

➤➤ What are the elements of a good relationship?

➤➤ Release someone who has hurt you to God so He can deal with them and you can move on.

➤➤ What does God's relational love look like in your life, and what does it mean to you?

PROCESS

_____

_____

_____

_____

_____

_____

_____

_____

_____

๛ Zephaniah ๛
CELEBRATORY LOVE

The LORD your God is in your midst, a mighty one who will save;
he will rejoice over you with gladness; he will quiet you by his love;
he will exult over you with loud singing.
Zephaniah 3:17

When my son was about three he decided he might just get a mind of his own. Since he had spent his first years being overwhelmingly compliant, you can imagine my surprise one day when I asked him to take his toys to his room and he flat out said no.

Um, excuse me? I turned and looked incredulously into his adorable hazel eyes thinking I absolutely could not have heard him correctly. But as he stared back, I saw it standing at attention in the mini creases between his eyebrows: defiance. Thankfully, Coop's toddler rebellion game was weak, and it only took one timeout for him to decide maybe he would return his talking cars to their garages. After his chair sit, he padded out of his room toward me. I'm sure he didn't expect me to be knelt down there with open arms. (It was a good parenting day.)

"Thank you! I'm so proud of you, buddy!" I gave him a big hug, a high-five and eleventy hundred kisses on his squishy, little cheeks. I know he could have put up a fight and made our tiny apartment a warzone, but he chose to take the discipline and obey.

Unfortunately, in the first two chapters of Zephaniah, we find the people of Judah doing exactly the opposite. They have rebelled against God and decided they will not heed the warnings of the prophet but will, instead, take their chances with continued disobedience.

Why do you think they would choose their defiance over God's instruction when they know what it will bring in the end?

I guess when we totally turn our backs on God, we can end up in a place where we don't believe what He says or that He's even real and able to speak at all.

We witness God's love and mercy through Zephaniah being sent as a cautionary messenger, but His love absolutely oozes over in His reaction with His restored people in *Zephaniah 3:14-20*.

Our scripture portion today takes place after Judah's discipline. At the "Last Day", or end of time, when Christ reigns, Israel will again be whole and fully submitted to Christ – the One, True God. Yes, there is discipline, but in the end, there will be obedience. And His response? Rejoicing and singing over them. Don't you love that visual? He's visibly excited.

In Acts 10, Peter learns from a God-given vision that the Gentiles (non-Jewish folk) are welcomed into God's kingdom. Hooray for us! As if that weren't enough, we read in Luke 15:7 that all of heaven rejoices over one person who comes into a saving relationship with Jesus. So, just as God will rejoice over the nation of Israel in the end days, He rejoices over you and me with that same kind of excited joy when we say yes to his offer of eternal salvation. It's almost impossible to imagine, isn't it? He looks at you and is genuinely overjoyed. That's CELEBRATORY love.

PICK and PRAY

➵ Is it difficult to imagine God celebrating your salvation? Draw a visual of how you imagine that to look.

➵ Thank God that He loves you so much that He is genuinely excited about spending eternity with you.

➵ What does God's celebratory love look like in your life, and what does it mean to you?

PROCESS

৵ Haggai ৻
PRESENT LOVE

"'I am with you' declares the LORD."
from Haggai 1:13

I know two chapters seems like a lot to read, but *Haggai 1 & 2* are really short. We're going to pull from them both, so if you read it all, you'll get more out of this chapter of study. Please go ahead and do so. I dare you!

It's a good read, isn't it? However, you may be thinking, *Wait. I thought they rebuilt the temple back in Ezra.* They did, but remember there was a break when they didn't build for a while.

When delayed in a project, how long does that delay have to be for you to become frustrated or discouraged?

The Israelites' cessation lasted close to 20 years, so it took some mighty prophets named Haggai and Zechariah to get them going again.[24] This little book is part of that story.

We can see in 1:2 that the people have just decided that right now is not the time to continue construction. However, "the word of the LORD" comes through Haggai in 1:3, and the command to recommence is given.

What is the reason for rebuilding given in 1:8?

The first temple was a wonder – beautiful to behold. But more than that, it was the center of worship and a visible representation of the presence of God. He wanted it reestablished for those very reasons.

Jump over to 1 Corinthians 6:19. What is our body called?

In the very next verse it goes on to say we are not our own and were bought with a price. That price was the blood of Jesus Christ. Because of His sacrifice for our sin, we can now become a cleansed vessel for God's presence and a representation of Him to the world around us. Isn't that completely unbelievable? It's a high calling but such an honor.

What declaration of the Lord in Haggai 2:13 spurred the people to go ahead and obey the command to build?

Because we are the temple of God, He goes with us everywhere we go. When He asks us for obedience, He is right there helping us. He empowers us to do what He commands. We don't ever have to do it alone.

In 2:5 and 9, we see another benefit of God remaining in us: less fear. More peace. In this hectic world full of fear-inducing stimuli, we can all use a little more of that.

God not only gently calls us into a relationship, but then He sticks around and accompanies us through every step He asks us to take. That's PRESENT love.

PICK and PRAY

➢ Is there something God has asked you to do that you have stopped? Don't be ashamed; restart!

➢ God's presence gives you peace. Invite Him into any area of anxiety.

➢ What does God's present love look like in your life, and what does it mean to you?

PROCESS

৵ Zechariah ৵

IMPARTIAL LOVE

"Thus says the LORD of hosts, 'Render true judgments, show kindness and mercy to one another, do not oppress the widow, the fatherless, the sojourner, or the poor, and let none of you devise evil against another in your heart.'"
Zechariah 7:9-10

Like most of the Old Testament prophets, in this book, Zechariah is speaking to the nation of Israel about repentance, the turning away from sin and back toward God. Though it is a message we may tire of hearing, it is one we are wise to continue to heed. Anytime we hear the voice of God urging us to come back to Him, we have traveled too far and are in danger. I pray we are quick to slam it in reverse every single time.

Zechariah's and Haggai's ministries were somewhat intertwined as they were both concerned with the rebuilding of the temple upon Israel's return from exile.[25] In our reading today, we get a clearer picture of Israel's condition before God let her be taken into that exile. Go ahead and read *Zechariah 7:8-14*.

According to verses 11-12, what caused the Lord to get angry enough to scatter them?

He had given them clear instructions for how He desired them to treat others, but they simply refused. Look back at verses 9-10. What did God want them to do?

It all seems reasonable, doesn't it? He simply wanted them to treat each other kindly and fairly. I'm not sure what would cause them to willingly oppress an orphan, but let's not judge. After all, I can't even count the number of times I have sneered at someone's sin only to have God expose the same or similar fault in my own heart. Let us never think we're above falling down again. We may be healed. We may be free. But we don't have it all together, and all our freedom is completely dependent on God's grace and faithfulness.

Though God paints a dismal picture of Israel's unfaithfulness through Zechariah, the bigger portrait revealed is a vibrant rendering of God's love for the disenfranchised. His desire is for the ethical and loving treatment of the foreign, poor, widowed, and orphaned. These people who might have been forgotten, discarded or are distrusted: God saw them all, and He loved them fully.

Nothing has changed today. That neighbor from a different culture? That prostitute on the corner? The drug addict begging for money at the intersection? God loves them as much as your pastor on the stage every Sunday. If we believe any differently, our version of the gospel has become works-based. Likewise, if we believe God enjoys keeping the company of the sweet church lady down the street but only tolerates our presence, our theology is skewed. God *is* love; therefore, He loves. It doesn't matter if we're "good" or "bad", affluent or poor, succeeding or failing. He loves us in all conditions.

Today, endeavor to simply accept this love He pours out on the least likely recipients – His undeserved love open to anyone who will receive it. That is IMPARTIAL love.

PICK and PRAY

➤➤ If it is difficult for you to accept that God loves us all equally, talk to Him about that.

➤➤ God's love for the foreign, poor, widowed, and orphan – which do you relate to? How so?

➤➤ What does God's impartial love look like in your life, and what does it mean to you?

PROCESS

_____

_____

_____

_____

_____

_____

_____

_____

_____

❧ *Malachi* ❧

CONSTANT LOVE

For I the LORD do not change; therefore you,
O children of Jacob, are not consumed.
(3:6)

We have reached the final book of the Old Testament! This is the last we hear from the people who lived before the era of Jesus Christ. So often, God is misportrayed as frothing with wrath and void of compassion in the Old Testament, so I have relished our time uncovering His love in this part of the Bible. I hope you have too.

Before we get to today's scripture, please read 1:2. What is the first thing God says to His people?

It reminds me of a parent sitting knee-to-knee with a disobedient child. He must rebuke and discipline, but he wants his little one to know she is deeply cared for before he says anything else. Today we are reading God's message to Israel, who has grown careless in her relationship with Him. They have married people of other faiths (which has drawn them away from their pure worship of Him), have neglected or polluted their tithes and offerings and generally robbed Him of the unadulterated worship He deserves. Out of the love He reveals in verse 2, He speaks our scripture portion today. Go ahead and give *Malachi 3:5-7* a read.

Verse 5 is no fun, but 6 is like ice cream on a melty August day. What does God say about Himself in this verse?

In a culture where promises are frequently half-hearted and people morph at the whim of their social media "likes", knowing that our God is unchanging is a stabilizing truth in a topsy-turvy world. In this context, God is reassuring Israel that His promises of returning and reestablishing His people still stand. Today, it means everything we read in God's Word is still true.

- You are forgiven and clean. (1 John 1:9)
- You are a new creation. (2 Corinthians 5:17)
- God will complete the work He has started in you. (Philippians 1:6)
- He has given you a spirit of love, power and self-control. (2 Timothy 1:7)
- He will use all things in your life for your good. (Romans 8:28)

- He loves you with an unfailing love. (Psalm 36:5-7)
- No one can snatch you out of God's hand. (John 10:29)
- He will never leave you. (Hebrews 13:5)
- He Himself will help you through life. (Hebrews 13:6)

I could go on and on; the promises of God are almost unending. Even though the Word of God was written thousands of years ago, it reveals a God who, today, still loves us deeply, makes promises birthed out of that love and never changes His mind about us. That is CONSTANT love.

PICK and PRAY

➤➤ What are you glad never changes about God? Why?

➤➤ Thank God that you never have to wonder how He feels or be afraid He will change His mind about you.

➤➤ What does God's constant love look like in your life, and what does it mean to you?

PROCESS

_____

_____

_____

_____

_____

_____

_____

_____

_____

LOVE THROUGHOUT

the

New
Testament

✀ *Matthew* ✀
GUIDING LOVE

But as he considered these things, behold, an angel of the Lord
appeared to him in a dream, saying, "Joseph, son of David, do not
fear to take Mary as your wife, for that which is conceived in her is
from the Holy Spirit."
Matthew 1:20

We did it! We made it through the Old Testament and are more than halfway through the entire Bible. If I could, I would give you a high five. Now, in the New Testament, we get to see God's love in a completely new way: through His Son Jesus. If you're not familiar with the difference between the Old and New Testaments, it's helpful to know the Old Testament is composed of church literature from before Jesus' ministry on earth, while the New Testament is all about His arrival, His work, and what happened after He died and returned to the Father. I'm excited for us to see the Father's love worked out tangibly through the hands of His Son.

A quality I love most about God is His vigilance. This characteristic used to unnerve me a bit. I guess because it seemed very creepy and stalkerish. Very hiding in the bushes and observing me from the darkish, you know? I mean, who wants someone to see all the most intimate parts of themselves? Nobody needs to know how much I think about queso or watch Netflix.

How do you feel about God seeing everything?

As I've come to see God is for us and only wants what's best for us, I now see His watchfulness as His diligent care. He's not policing like a sheriff looking for lawbreakers. His attentiveness is more like a counselor who is guiding us toward health and wholeness. Toward holiness. It's comforting now to know that this God, who loves so intensely, sees when we're about to turn down a road that leads to heartache or darkness and cares enough to step in. Today you get to see this tendency in Matthew. Go ahead and read *Matthew 1:18-25*, please.

Jesus' life here on earth begins just like the rest of us: in His mother's womb. However, what is shocking (don't let the surprise escape you out of familiarity) is that Mary is a virgin and engaged to Joseph. This has scandal written all over it. To Joseph, Mary must look like an adulteress who has broken her marital vows by having sex with someone else. He has the legal right to divorce her and demand retribution. This would bring Mary great public shame. Joseph can also opt to leave her quietly, forfeiting any monetary restitution, so Mary's exposure is reduced and her shame minimized. He has a decision to make. He decides to divorce her privately to save her from more public humiliation. Joseph is a good man, and he thinks he is doing the right thing as he lays down his head for a peaceful night's sleep.

Then he has his dream.

Just think what Joseph would have missed if he had left Mary. In all his reasoning and striving to get it right, he would have walked away from God's will and completely missed having a front row seat to the birth and life of the Christ. God interrupts Joseph's life before he makes a life-altering mistake, and He does the same for us. He sees us and desires to help us follow and obey Him. He doesn't abandon us to the dark or relish our confusion. He watches our life and redirects us when we're going off-course. That's GUIDING love.

PICK and PRAY

➟ When have you thought God might have stepped in and saved you from a big mistake? Thank Him.

➟ Spend some time praying about the decisions you have to make in the near future.

➟ What does God's guiding love look like in your life, and what does it mean to you?

PROCESS

☙ Mark ❧

WELCOMING LOVE

But when Jesus saw it, he was indignant and said to them, "Let the children come to me; do not hinder them, for to such belongs the kingdom of God."
Mark 10:14

Teenagers are the coolest people on the planet. Don't believe me? Ask one to show you their favorite funny meme, and then ask for their thoughts on a current political topic. My guess is you will chuckle and then be caught off guard by their depth of thinking about current cultural trends. They're hilarious and quirky and complex all at the same time. Put me in a room full of 'em, and I'll gladly stay parked right there and call it my happy place.

I think Jesus feels the same way. Check out *Mark 10:13-16*.

What's your first reaction? Do you resonate more with Jesus or the disciples in this story?

Don't beat yourself up if you and the disciples could be buds. Kids aren't everyone's cup of tea. Teens are my thing – not the littles so much. You'll hear no shame from me. But don't you love Jesus's reaction to the disciples' chastisement?

"Let the children come to me; do not hinder them."

Then He reaches out and physically touches blessing upon them. Can't you feel the tenderness and compassion He feels for them? Though this passage is more about having a childlike faith, we can't escape the fact that Jesus welcomed the children, spent time with them and hugged all over them. He had a genuinely deep affection for them.

He looked at the ones who were seen as annoying or unimportant, who had been shoved to the side and drew them into His arms. He gave them His undivided attention. He bestowed dignity.

Who in your world, in your neighborhood, in your school, maybe even in your own family might be feeling unimportant or left out? Or is it you?

God knows. He sits with the lonely student in the lunchroom who eats alone with earbuds in and head buried in phone. He notices the mom at home with preschoolers wondering if she will ever have another adult relationship. He holds dear the soldier overseas who wonders if what he's doing even matters. He accompanies the college freshman who is struggling to find a place to fit in. He sees.

And He cares.

When we feel discarded or looked over, there is One who welcomes us and has open arms for us always. He will never reject us or pass us over. He delights in us and speaks words of dignity over us. Today let's accept them as truth and be people who speak those same kinds of words back into our areas of influence. This is how we change the world one word at a time. We open our arms to the forgotten and love them the way Jesus does: with a WELCOMING love.

PICK and PRAY

➳ Have you ever felt unimportant or discarded? Give that circumstance to Jesus and let Him speak worth and dignity over you.

➳ Who in your life needs to know they are valued?

➳ What does God's welcoming love look like in your life, and what does it mean to you?

PROCESS

TRUTHFUL LOVE

But the Lord answered her, "Martha, Martha, you are anxious and troubled about many things, but one thing is necessary. Mary has chosen the good portion, which will not be taken away from her.
Luke 10:41-42

If awards were given for spotless, well-organized homes, my in-laws would take home the gold. In my 20 years of being part of their family, there has been exactly one time I have seen dust in their house, and this was when they both had surgery within the same month. Their home is refreshingly tidy and always peaceful to spend time in. And you know what? They never have to spend 10 minutes looking for a pen. It, like everything else, has a place to belong and always makes it back home. I envy their ability to maintain this level of order. Worked into my daily schedule are search times for my glasses and keys and kicking aside the dust bunnies that skitter across my hardwoods. If they didn't love me so much I would worry about being a disappointment.

Today we read about Martha – a woman who lets her need to tidy get the best of her. Go ahead and read *Luke 10:38-42*.

There is nothing wrong with having a home ready for guests. Some of my friends have the gift of hospitality and their homes are lovely. However, how does Jesus describe Martha after she complains about Mary's lack of help?

Martha's emotional state was keeping her from sitting down with Jesus and hearing what He might have to say to her. Her anxious mind made frantic hands.

What does Philippians 4:6-7 say to do with our worry and anxiety? What is the result if we do?

Isn't that a wonderful promise? We spend so much time searching for ways to calm ourselves and relieve the frenzy that seems to be a constant companion in this culture. Who knew the answer was so simple?

The answer may be simple, but it is not natural. Instead of obtaining the peace she could have received from Jesus, Martha takes to preparing her home to entertain

Him. She then becomes distracted, irritated and frustrated with her family.

And Jesus calls her out.

However, you'll notice Jesus speaks gently. He doesn't embarrass her or shame her. He doesn't call down fire from Heaven. He is merely honest about her condition and its effect on her. He is truthful, but He is also tender. He's able to be both.

Sometimes we mistake telling the truth with being hurtful. We think being real means being rude. That simply isn't accurate. Sometimes the most loving thing we can do is take our cue from Jesus and speak the truth with compassion. Jesus *is* love and He was always honest. That's TRUTHFUL love.

PICK and PRAY

➤➤ Do you resonate more with Mary or Martha? Why?

➤➤ What is one thing you could do differently to foster more of the peace found in Jesus?

➤➤ What does God's truthful love look like in your life, and what does it mean to you?

PROCESS

❧ John ❧

FREEING LOVE

Jesus stood up and said to her, "Woman, where are they? Has no
one condemned you?" She said, "No one, Lord." And Jesus said,
"Neither do I condemn you; go, and from now on sin no more."
John 8:10-11

This may sound weird since our scripture is about adultery today, but the 11 verses in *John 8:1-11* are some of my favorite verses in the entirety of the Bible. Top 3.

#1. The crucifixion, because it saved my soul.
#2. The resurrection, because it enabled me to have a relationship with Jesus.

#3. This scripture right here. That may sound dramatic, but I am what I am. I came to terms with my overblown emotions a long time ago. Roll with me.

What's one of your favorite scriptures and why? If you're new to the Bible, what have you heard so far in this study that you have liked?

The scene opens with Jesus teaching the people at the temple. I envision Him sitting among interested seekers and genuine searchers, when suddenly, the reverent air is broken with a kick up of dust and a woman hurled into the middle of the gathering. She is most likely barely clothed, if at all, since she has just been caught in adultery. The religious leaders, who do not believe Jesus is the Messiah, have brought her in to try to trip Him up. You see, the law of Moses stated adulterous women must be stoned, but the leaders knew Jesus was bent on grace and were hoping He would extend some to her so they could catch Him breaking the law.

Lean in. We need so badly to hear our Lord's response to shame.

After diverting their attention from the humiliated woman by bending down and writing in the sand, He stands up and says,

> *"Let him who is without sin among you be the first*
> *to throw a stone at her."*

And can you believe it? Every single one of those finger pointers dropped their stones and went home! Conviction has a sneaky way of making even the most judgy a little more forgiving. As wonderful as that interaction is, it's not really why I love this scripture with my whole heart. It's what Jesus says next.

Jesus stood up and said to her, "Woman, where are they? Has no one condemned you?" She said, "No one, Lord." And Jesus said, "Neither do I condemn you; go, and from now on sin no more."

Jesus knew exactly what she was. He knew her sin and saw her at her exposed worst. And instead of picking up a stone to condemn her, he clothed her with words of love. Jesus is not about shame. Never will be.

There is therefore now no condemnation for those who are in Christ Jesus.
Romans 8:1

This is a sobering reminder to us on those days when we relentlessly beat ourselves up. If the God of the universe tilts up our chin, looks us in the eye and says, "I don't condemn you", then what are we doing berating ourselves? No matter what we think when we look in the mirror, He is our creator and His opinion is the correct one. If He says we are forgiven, we are. If He says we have dignity and worth, then we do. He removes our shame. That's FREEING love.

PICK and PRAY

➤ What do you need to lay down at Jesus's feet and finally stop condemning yourself for?

➤ Write out Romans 8:1 on an index card and start memorizing it.

➤ What does God's freeing love look like in your life, and what does it mean to you?

PROCESS

_____

_____

_____

_____

_____

_____

_____

_____

_____

RELEVANT LOVE

They were all filled and equipped with the Holy Spirit and were inspired to speak in tongues – empowered by the Spirit to speak in languages they had never learned!
Acts. 2:4 TPT

Growing up one of my favorite Christmas traditions was opening one gift on Christmas Eve. The majority of our yuletide haul was reserved for the following morning, but a few hours before we retired on the 24th, my sister and I were allowed to unwrap one goodie. I received some fun gifts throughout the years, but there was a span of about three years when all my heightened anticipation would come crashing down in bitter disappointment as I tore into something like an umbrella or brief underwear. When I was about 10, I received a swath of fabric with a Simplicity robe pattern laid atop. Mom's intentions were sweet in letting me know she would be hand-sewing me a fuzzy robe, but she didn't get the grateful reaction she deserved. Don't worry. I forgave her the next morning as I hugged my new Cabbage Patch doll with chestnut braids.

In *Acts 2:1- 41* we see an astonishing gift given to mankind – the Holy Spirit. Many of us know about Him, but we're not quite sure what He does. Check out what's on His daily rotation of tasks.

He lives inside every believer – Acts 2:38; 1 Cor. 6:19; Eph. 1:13

He helps us, teaches us, and reminds us of what He's taught us – Neh. 9:20; John 14:26

He intercedes for us when we don't know what to pray – Rom. 8:26

He gives us power to accomplish His purpose – Acts 1:8, 2:17-18; 4:31

He gives us gifts to serve people – 1 Cor. 12

He washes, sanctifies and justifies us – 1 Cor. 6:11

He convicts us of sin – John 16:8

He produces love, joy, peace, patience, kindness, goodness, faithfulness, gentleness and self-control in us – Gal. 5:22-23

He guides us – Rom. 8:14

He reveals spiritual truths to us – John 16:12-15; 1 Cor. 2:9-13

He transforms us into the image of God – 2 Cor. 3:18

He frees us – 2 Cor. 3:17

That's a pretty spectacular gift – one that keeps on giving! We need not take this gift who lives inside us lightly. Some see Him as irrelevant to their daily lives and ignore His existence. However, what He does matters. His jobs are numerous, and they are paramount to our God experience. As we yield to His leadership, we will find ourselves more fulfilled, equipped, and free to enjoy God. That's RELEVANT love.

PICK and PRAY

➤ Which action of the Holy Spirit is your favorite? Why?

➤ What would it look like for you to give the Holy Spirit more control in your life?

➤ What does God's relevant love look like in your life, and what does it mean to you?

PROCESS

‿ Romans ‿

EQUIPPING LOVE

Having gifts that differ according to the grace given to us, let us use them
from Romans 12:6

Can you imagine going to a fine dining restaurant only to have your meal prepared by a heart doctor? Or vise versa – to have the chef do surgery on your heart? Either way, the results could be deadly. Although both are skilled with cutting utensils, I prefer they operate in their area of gifting! In *Romans 12:3-8* we see a different kind of gifting, and you might be pleased at the recipients.

Yesterday we talked about the gift of the Holy Spirit. Today we see that He is the gift that keeps on giving – the giver of our gifts. Something else cool? Check out 1 Peter 4:10. According to Peter, which believers get these gifts?

If you have committed your life to Jesus, the Holy Spirit lives in you and has given you at least one "spiritual gift". There are quite a few of these listed in the New Testament. You can find them all in 1 Corinthians 12, Romans 12, Ephesians 4 and 1 Peter 4.

God has a purpose for your life. If He didn't, He would have snatched you right up the moment you gave your life to Him. He left you here for a reason, and it has everything to do with His kingdom. You may have a special skill set and be the best in your chosen field, but how do you affect eternity with it all?

Your spiritual gifting is the answer.

What if you are a CPA but have the gift of encouragement? You could be the accountant in the office who is always speaking life over your coworkers. Maybe you are a stay-at-home mom but have the gift of administration. You could volunteer to help a ministry with their office work. We creative types need people like you! There are a million different ways your gifts can help the kingdom.

To what do verses 4 and 5 compare the church?

Just as a human body has different parts with different functions, the church is comprised of many, varied types of people with many, varied types of gifts. Everybody has an important role. Just as the body could not function well without a heart or kidneys, the body of Christ operates optimally only when everyone is playing their personal part. Do you know what part you play?

Rest assured. God absolutely has a field of expertise for you – a place for you to do ministry. It's all around you. It's populated by the people in your office, your home, your neighborhood and your school. It's the guy at the grocery store and the woman who prepares your taxes. It's the teacher or professor in the front of the classroom. It's everywhere. That sounds a bit daunting, but then we remember that God not only gives us a call to ministry, He cares enough to also supply us with the gifting we need to do what He's asked us to do. He calls us and then sends us out fully prepared and enabled by His Spirit. That's EQUIPPING love.

PICK and PRAY

➤ Take a spiritual gifts test online, and then ask God what He wants to do with your gifting.

➤ Who has God asked you to minister to but you didn't recognize that until right now?

➤ What does God's equipping love look like in your life, and what does it mean to you?

PROCESS

❧ 1 Corinthians ❧
COMPLETE LOVE

Love is patient and kind; love does not envy or boast; it is not
arrogant
1 Corinthians 13:4

If you've ever been to a wedding, you've probably heard "the love chapter" of the Bible. It's a regular nuptial menu item. Go ahead and give it a read at *1 Corinthians 13:1-8*.

It's nice, right? Everybody loves love, but after attending ceremony after ceremony and hearing the same scriptures, I daresay I tire of hearing it. I start to tune out as soon as I hear the words "Love is". *Oh here we go again*, I think.

1 John 4:8 to the rescue! What does it say God is?

He *is* love. We'll talk more about this when we get to the 1 John chapter. Can't wait! For now, though, let's think about God, love and 1 Corinthians. If God *is* love, when we read the love chapter, we can replace all the places it says *love* with the word *God.*

God is patient.

God is kind.

God does not envy or boast.

God is not arrogant.

God is not rude.

God does not insist on His own way (we have choice).

God is not irritable or resentful.

You get the idea. Go back and read our scripture portion again, and this time insert God's name everywhere it says *love.*

What quality of God from your reading is your favorite? Why?

We encounter a plethora of ideas in our culture about God and what He does or does not do, think and feel. If any of it goes against the picture He paints of Himself in this chapter, it is simply a lie.

You'll notice that nothing we do matters if we don't love people. We're not eternally effective if we don't actively care about them. I wonder if that's why God loves the way He does. If He came at us with fire and brimstone screaming about going to Hell and then removed Himself to a place far from us, we probably wouldn't respond by drawing near to Him. Thankfully, He calls us gently to Himself, is patient with our messiness, speaks words of adoration over us, refuses to rejoice over our failings but, instead, endures all things with us. Forever. His crazy brand of multifaceted love goes on eternally. That's COMPLETE love.

PICK and PRAY

- What picture of God have you had that has been inaccurate? Repent and surrender it.
- Pray about and thank God for your favorite quality of His from this chapter.
- What does God's complete love look like in your life, and what does it mean to you?

PROCESS

✍ 2 Corinthians ✍

RESTORATIVE LOVE

Blessed be the God and Father of our Lord Jesus Christ, the Father
of mercies and God of all comfort
2 Corinthians 1:3

Suffering is no fun. No matter how many times you tell me that we learn through pain, I will never sign up for it. Ever. Given the choice, I will choose safety and happiness and kitties and rainbows every single time. I'm just not built for tough times, man.

What does John 16:33 say we will have in this world?

Yep. Trouble. Anybody else singing Taylor Swift right now? Just me? Anyway, you'll notice it says we *will* have trouble, not we *might*. I'm not a fan of that sentence. I know the spiritually mature thing to do is to be thankful for difficulties since that's where we grow, but it takes my entire reserve of will power to push those words out of my mouth. Even when I do, my feelings are rebellious and don't follow instructions. I would rather not think about it at all, really.

However, scripture like *2 Corinthians 1:1-11* forces us to consider suffering and what it's all about. Go ahead and read, please.

What are your first thoughts when you read that?

I'm conflicted myself, and I'll show you why. Take a look at the original meanings of some of the words we just read.

Blessed (v.3) – used of God only; worthy of praise

Mercies (v. 3) – compassion, pity, a deep feeling about someone's difficulty or misfortune

Affliction (v. 4) – Internal pressure that causes someone to feel confined

Sufferings (v. 5) – the capacity and privilege of experiencing deep emotion
(all portions taken from BibleHub.com)

Our trials are described as constricting, inward and deep. I get that. However, they are also called a privilege, and God is characterized as worthy of praise in all of this hurting business. What's the deal there?

The answer may lie in God's feelings for our *deep* emotional sufferings also being *deep*. There's a kinship there; He meets us at the intensity at which we need Him. According to verse 4, He also comforts us. So, His deep emotions move Him to meaningful action. Okay, we do like that, but it still doesn't explain why suffering is a privilege.

What does verse 4 say we can do with the comfort God gives us?

There it is. When God allows us to suffer, He entrusts us with the privilege of transferring His comfort to others who are hurting. What a high, holy calling. If we must suffer, I'm thankful we have a God who pulls us in close and then heals us so thoroughly that we can speak His love out of that newly mended place. That's RESTORATIVE love.

PICK and PRAY

➤ When something is hurt, what does it take to restore it? Think of God in that light.

➤ Thank God for His desire to comfort you.

➤ What does God's restorative love look like in your life, and what does it mean to you?

PROCESS

⨀ Galatians ⨀
REFRESHING LOVE

Know then that it is those of faith who are the sons of Abraham.
Galatians 3:7

I'm a professional writer, but I'm also a high school teacher. Best. Job. Ever. My first years in the classroom were spent instructing students how to interpret literature and compose grammatically correct (and maybe even eloquent) sentences. We analyzed poetry, acted out Shakespeare and created ingenious visual displays of our literary prowess. Much of the time, they actually had fun! However, there always came that dreaded time of year when my students must write a research paper. They hated it, but I tried to ease their pain by giving them well-explained instructions, step-by-step examples and due dates. My goal was to be so clear they could see through me. Nevertheless, I always had those few students who seemed to be allergic to my directions. They tuned me out and stuffed the instruction packet deep into the bowels of their backpacks where it was only exposed to light on due dates. It would usually emerge looking like a bear had taken a long winter's nap on it. Unfortunately, their insistence on doing it their way earned them a lower grade than they would have received if they simply would have looked at and followed my instructions. They made it so much harder on themselves, those precious, 6-foot-tall punkins! Please read *Galatians 3:1-9* and see another group of folks trying to accomplish an important task with their own recipes.

According to 3:1-3, how are the Galatians trying to "perfect" themselves?

When we think of the word *perfect* in our modern language, we think of being without any type of blemish. However, the meaning of the word in this ancient context is more about reaching completion or maturity. It's what the church calls sanctification – becoming more like Jesus.

The Galatians are being swayed by surrounding arguments that they need to follow the law of Moses in order to be better Christ-followers – that Jesus alone is somehow not enough.[26] Paul refutes that notion by reminding them that the simple gospel message they were given in the beginning – the original instructions – had not changed. Just as they were saved by faith, their sanctification comes by the same method: not in their own power, but through His work in them.

Many of us want to follow our own instructions for how to walk with Jesus and become more Christ-like. We think we must vigilantly watch our language, watch our attitudes and watch what we watch. All that is beneficial, but if it's our focus, we've got it backward. Jesus didn't come to save us so we could continue trying to be "good". He came and saved us so we would know we're already good through Him. We don't have to strive to be better. His directions are short: love Him and love people. He'll do the work of making us more like Himself.

Here's the great thing about that truth. It frees us up to stop looking inward and begin looking out. When we stop trying to fix ourselves and instead walk in the grace Christ died to give us, people just may be able to see in us Paul's message from our focus verse: they don't have to clean up their act. They get grace with Jesus. We become a member of God's family, a son of Abraham, through faith alone. No need to be perfect. No expectation to have all the answers. We get to give out the same gift we received – an introduction to the God who wants us to rest in His love and grace. We are loved because we are His. Period. That is REFRESHING love.

PICK and PRAY

➤➤ Is there anything you're tempted to add to the simple message of salvation?

➤➤ In what ways can you let God grow you instead of you trying to make it happen?

➤➤ What does God's refreshing love look like in your life, and what does it mean to you?

PROCESS

❧ *Ephesians* ❧
RESURRECTING LOVE

But God, being rich in mercy, because of the great love with which
he loved us, even when we were dead in our trespasses, made us
alive together with Christ – by grace you have been saved – and
raised us up with him and seated us with him in the heavenly places
in Christ Jesus
Ephesians 2:4-6

I kill plants. I don't mean to. I dream of having a lovely garden full of vibrantly colored blooms like my brother-in-law, but I'm relegated to the world of cacti and succulents. Since they thrive in dry, arid places like my oft-forgotten windowsill, we get along swimmingly. I wish I could say the same for the beautiful orchid and lily plants my husband has given me over the years. Unfortunately, his efforts to love me with floral gifts usually end with me feeling shamed by a neglected flower carcass. He now buys me lattes.

Over and over again in the Bible, spiritual realities are explained to us using horticulture references: types of soil, seeds and planting, watering and growing, just to name a few. It also employs language about the human life cycle with terms such as *born again, life, death, mature,* and *faith like a child. Ephesians 2:1-10* is a great example. Go ahead and give it a quick read.

Isn't it some of the best stuff you've ever read? According to 2:1, what were we considered when we did not know Christ?

Dead as the potted plants on my back porch. Lifeless. Before we make that fateful decision to trust Jesus for our salvation and commit to live our lives for Him, we are destined for death: eternal separation from God. Forever. Never-ending. But then come verses 4 and 5 – some of the most beautiful words in all of the New Testament. Fill in the following blanks.

_____ _____, *being* _____ *in* _____, *because of*
the _____ _____ *with which he loved us, even when*
we were _____ *in our trespasses, made us*
_____ *together with* _____. *(ESV)*

Can you see how drastic the change is in us when we finally accept the grace God is offering and turn control over to Him?

- We are no longer controlled by our _____ (vs. 3)
- We have been raised up and seated with _____ (vs. 6)
- We have new purpose – to walk in the good _____ He prepared for us (vs. 10)

We don't have to call the shots anymore. There's freedom in that. We also have a new position in the very presence of God. There's worth in that. We have a mission in this world. There's purpose in that. That moment we decide our lives will be lived for Christ encompasses more than just being saved from hell. His love and mercy brings what was dead back to thriving life! Real life. That's RESURRECTING love.

PICK and PRAY

➤➤ Thank God for giving you a new, purposeful, joyful life in Him.

➤➤ What does it mean to be saved by grace, not works?

➤➤ What does God's resurrecting love look like in your life, and what does it mean to you?

PROCESS

_____

_____

_____

_____

_____

_____

_____

_____

_____

_____

❧ *Philippians* ❧
STEADYING LOVE

I can do all things through him who strengthens me.
Philippians 4:13

Several years ago, I got separated from most of my best friends by life and moves. One lives three hours away, another four and still another twelve. We're all over the place, and distance creates a challenge to friendships. As the days and miles click by, it gets easier and easier to lose touch. There have been moments when I realize I have forgotten a birthday or have neglected to check in when I knew one of them was facing a struggle. Distance makes relationships difficult.

One facet of God's love I cherish most is His close proximity and we get to witness its effects in *Philippians 4:10-13*.

In chapter one, we learn Paul is writing this letter from prison. He is no stranger to the chains, having been imprisoned numerous times for preaching the gospel in cities that found the idea offensive. The fact that Paul is sitting in a dark, dank cell, shackled in captivity, makes his words of contentment astonishing.

List all the different circumstances in which Paul has learned to find contentment.

We may not find ourselves without food, but we might feel hungry for love or peace. We may not consider ourselves to be "in need" because we are living in a home with a car outside and clothes in our closet. But there are countless things we may be without: a substantial paycheck, joy, health, self-control, friendship or peace. Maybe we fall on the other end of the spectrum. We look at our lives and know we have more than enough – relationally, physically, emotionally and financially – but we still feel an emptiness.

In what area of your life do you find it difficult to find contentment?

Somehow, Paul has found the secret to having contentment no matter what situation he may face, and we see it right there in verse 13: a classic.

I can do all things through Him who strengthens me.

This verse has been used for everything from a high school letter jacket patch to a declaration for triumph over tragedy. However, the context in which it's being used is in the area of contentedness. It's not at all about God giving you the strength to be the best in your chosen field (though He can absolutely do that). It's an encouragement that we are not controlled by our circumstances but are instead strengthened by Christ to be at peace in those circumstances.

Whether times are wonderful or waning, seasons are salty or sweet, the key to not being at the mercy of any of it is the constant, close presence of Christ.

As we walk hand-in-hand with Him, He gives us the power to turn our eyes from the ever-changing temporary to find an unwavering peace in Him. That is STEADYING love.

PICK and PRAY

➤➤ Name the areas in which you find it difficult to be content and give them to God. Ask Him for His strength to find your peace in Him alone.

➤➤ How have you seen that God is in close proximity to you? Thank Him.

➤➤ What does God's steadying love look like in your life, and what does it mean to you?

PROCESS

❧ Colossians ❧

SAVING LOVE

And you, who were dead in your trespasses and the uncircumcision of your flesh, God made alive together with him, having forgiven us all our trespasses, by canceling the record of debt that stood against us with its legal demands This he set aside, nailing it to the cross.
Colossians 2:13-14

Though I would have called myself a Christian as a teen, I didn't really start following Jesus until I was 27. Consequently, my twenties were . . . let's just call them wild and move on. I thank God regularly for saving my nappy little soul. Lord knows I didn't deserve it. One night in particular I got pulled over for speeding on a major street in Houston. I instantly remembered I had a warrant out for my arrest for not paying a ticket. *Maybe if I'm happy, he won't look up my record,* I thought. As I peered into my side mirror and watched the mammoth leather boots of an HPD officer draw closer, my hands and eyes betrayed my show of strength by leaking their cowardly salty liquid. Sweat and tears do not a confident appearance make.

"License and registration, please." *Ugh. Here we go. I'm getting thrown in the clink.* It didn't take long for Officer Life Destroyer to return and announce what I already knew. "Miss Abrams, you have a warrant out for your arrest." More tears. I was mentally preparing my case when he added, "I'll tell you what. If your friend here doesn't have a warrant out for his arrest, I'll let you go. But you have to promise you'll get this taken care of immediately."

I've been reprieved! Saved from the indignity of an orange jumpsuit! Thankfully, and now that I think about it, amazingly, my friend did not have a warrant out on this particular day. After receiving a warning from Officer My Hero, I rolled back into traffic unbelieving that I had been caught but let go with no punishment. The authorities were good to me that day.

In *Colossians 2:6-15*, we see Jesus referred to as the head of all authority. Maybe He whispered in my officer's ear that day, who knows. Go ahead and give it a read.

There is no one who is not under Jesus' reign. All things were made by Him, through Him and for Him.[27] That includes you and me. No matter what we believe, we are not our own bosses.

Why would it be dangerous to think we are our own authority?

One reason: it can blind us to the need for another authority. We reject anyone, God or not, who is trying to claim ownership of us. Unfortunately, when we do that to Christ, there is a devastating consequence. According to 2:13, what is it?

That means when we choose to live life apart from Christ, we are left with death: eternal separation from Him. Forever in the complete darkness that we chose.

Thank Him, a little like my HPD officer, Jesus saw our punishment looming and chose to offer forgiveness instead. In that one beautiful weekend when He allowed Himself to be nailed to a cross and then rose from the grave, He paid the price for our authority issue Himself and gave us a way to spend eternity in His presence. That's SAVING love. Let's not forget the price.

PICK and PRAY

➤➤ Thank God for the sacrifice He made in order to secure your salvation.

➤➤ What has been the biggest change in your life since your salvation, or what would you like to see changed if you decide to accept Jesus' salvation for you?

➤➤ What does God's saving love look like in your life, and what does it mean to you?

PROCESS

_____

_____

_____

_____

_____

_____

_____

_____

_____

_____

PERFECT LOVE

*Now may our God and Father himself, and our Lord Jesus, direct
our way to you, and may the Lord make you increase and abound in
love for one another and for all, as we do for you*
1 Thessalonians 3:11 – 12

A staple of the American comedy diet is family. We love to watch fictional families fumble through scenarios like Sammy's first date or little Wanda's affinity for smelly stray cats. One of my most loved TV families has to be the Banks crew of *The Fresh Prince of Bel-Air* fame. My favorite character, of course, is their teen nephew Will. Though I always laugh at his crazy antics, one of the best plot lines of the show is his relationship with Uncle Phil. About every three weeks or so, Uncle Phil ends up standing in the middle of the den confused and at his wit's end with Will. Despite his exasperation, though, Uncle Phil always handles Will with sensitivity, love and an understanding of the difficult situation from which Will came. He is a good dad, after all. He simply wants Will and his own two children to grow to be responsible, independent people who feel loved, important and empowered.

Unfortunately, most people don't grow up with a dad like Phillip Banks. His character is unrealistic, really. We are all raised with real people with real failings and weaknesses. Some of us grow up with abuse and some with no idea who our father is at all. So, when we read a verse like our focus verse today, we may feel emotions ranging from confusion to downright hatred. There seems to be no way to comprehend God as a father if you have a dad who is imperfect at best and abusive or absent at worst.

Lord, help us get it.

Let's look at *1 Thessalonians 3:6-13*. In the last three verses, God is called our Father twice. What does that mean, exactly? Romans 8:15 helps us understand.

*For you did not receive the spirit of slavery to fall back into fear, but you have
received the Spirit of adoption as sons, by whom we cry, "Abba! Father!"*

We are hand-picked and adopted in perfect love – a love that drives out fear and frees an enslaved spirit. Imagine the most perfect father choosing *you* to bring into his family to love and cherish. That kind of action would have long-lasting, powerful consequences.

Loving Relationship – He would love unconditionally and intentionally pursue a relationship with you. He would love you, not for what you do, but simply because you're you.

Forgiveness – He would show you your sins but then forgive you and gently help you choose differently next time.

Identity – You would move from being alone to being his child. You would always have a place to belong and a person who cherishes and welcomes you.

Freedom – A good father protects, guides, nurtures and instills dignity. Therefore, you would be free from feelings such as fear, confusion, and insignificance.

This is the Father you have – a daddy who chose you on purpose, who continues to intentionally love and help you and who frees and forgives you. His love is mature and complete – lacking nothing and never changing. That's PERFECT love.

PICK and PRAY

➤ What does it mean to you that you have been specifically chosen and adopted by God?
➤ How has God shown you sensitivity, love and understanding?
➤ What does God's perfect love look like in your life, and what does it mean to you?

PROCESS

_____

_____

_____

_____

_____

_____

_____

_____

❧ 2 Thessalonians ❧

SOOTHING LOVE

This is evidence of the righteous judgment of God, that you may be considered worthy of the kingdom of God, for which you are also suffering – since indeed God considers it just to repay with affliction those who afflict you, and to grant relief to you who are afflicted as well as to us, when the Lord Jesus is revealed from heaven with his mighty angels
2 Thessalonians 1:5-7

Today, we are starting off by reading *2 Thessalonians 1:5-12*. To a believer doing her best to walk with Christ in a world that seems hell bent on defaming Him and His people, its words are like a soothing balm on an open wound.

We don't normally read scripture about the coming judgment and find comfort, and here, there *is* a reason to grieve. Unfortunately, there will be many people who choose to reject Christ's offer of salvation and suffer an eternal separation from Him because of that. We mourn for them and do our best to love them into God's arms until the day He comes back. And pray. We pray our hearts out for them.

Any type of solace we get from a passage of scripture like this comes from words like those found in 1:5. What is the evidence of God's righteous judgment according to this verse?

Worthy. Every time I hear that word spoken over us, it comforts me like nothing else. We are worthy to inherit eternity in God's presence. Everyone is – even the people who don't want it. Jesus died a gruesome death on a torturous cross to give us that value. If anyone – *anyone* – ever doubts their worth, Jesus hangs on the cross saying, "I'm doing this for you. You are worth My death. Accept My gift. I want you to spend eternity with Me." But He is a gentleman and will not force Himself into your life. You have the choice to choose Him or not.

What does 1:7 say the Thessalonians will be granted upon His return?

The church in Thessalonica was undergoing persecution, and Paul is reassuring them that it will not last forever. Relief is coming. Even if they perish at its hands, it will not go on forever.

107

Then I saw a new heaven and a new earth, for the first heaven and the first earth had passed away, and the sea was no more. And I saw the holy city, new Jerusalem, coming down out of heaven from God, prepared as a bride adorned for her husband. And I heard a loud voice from the throne saying, "Behold, the dwelling place of God is with man. He will dwell with them, and they will be his people, and God himself will be with them as their God. He will wipe away every tear from their eyes, and death shall be no more, neither shall there be mourning, nor crying, nor pain anymore, for the former things have passed away." (Rev. 21:1-4)

Though we may suffer, though our days may get tough, God cares enough to count us worthy of the relief found in eternal life with Him. He even paid the ultimate price to give it to us. All we have to do is say yes, and we are assured a day with no more darkness is coming. That's SOOTHING love.

PICK and PRAY

➻ What do you feel knowing that there will be an end to the suffering?

➻ Thank God for providing you with worth and life.

➻ What does God's soothing love look like in your life, and what does it mean to you?

PROCESS

_____

_____

_____

_____

_____

_____

_____

_____

❧ 1 Timothy ☙
EMPOWERING LOVE

The saying is trustworthy and deserving of full acceptance, that
Christ Jesus came into the world to save sinners, of whom I am the
foremost.
1 Timothy 1:15

Have you ever had a moment when you came face-to-face with who you really are? Maybe it was a cutting thought that intruded upon your normally sweet mindset or a verbal assault that seemed to sucker punch someone in its own power. For me, my awakening comes when my husband mumbles, "Wow," with a look like he's been thumped between the eyeballs. This usually happens when he dares speak to me before 7 a.m. There's no guarantee of meek and mild if you try to speak words at my face before I've given Jesus a chance to make me nice. I am humbled by the sin that still tromps around inside my brain after all these years following Jesus.

I wonder when Paul's realization of his ongoing imperfection dawned on him. Was it on that road to Damascus when Jesus showed up and revealed Himself to be God and Paul to be a violent, misdirected murderer?[28] Maybe. Or could it have been when he heatedly argued with co-laborers like Peter[29] and Barnabas[30]? Possibly. My guess is Paul realized he was no angel just like the rest of us – in the everyday moments of living alongside other people. Go ahead and read *1 Timothy 1:12-17* keeping an eye out for exactly what Paul thinks of himself.

This man wrote the majority of the New Testament and is the reason the gospel was spread as widely as it was so early. Most Christians look up to him as a pillar of the church, and here he calls himself the chief of sinners? Yikes. That doesn't give the rest of us much hope, does it?

Or does it? Read verses 12-14 again, and fill in the missing words.

I thank him who has given me strength, Christ Jesus our Lord, because he judged

me _____ , *appointing me to his* _____ ,

though formerly I was a _____ ,

_____ , *and insolent*

_____ . *But I received* _____ *because I*

had acted ignorantly in unbelief, and the _____ *of our Lord*

overflowed for me with the faith and love that are in Christ Jesus.

Paul, the self-proclaimed chief of sinners, informs us that Jesus saw his faithful heart, showed him mercy and gave him a place of impactful service – in spite of his past and present sinfulness.

Have you ever felt disqualified or rejected because of something in your life? Yeah, me too. Keep that thing in mind as you remember what Paul says next.

In verse 16, Paul presents a truth that is paradigm-shifting if we can get it settled down deep in our core: God shows this mercy to Paul as an example to those who would follow in his faith footsteps in the future – those who would also choose Jesus. That's us!

You may feel that Paul's got nothing on your past or present sin level. Because of your feeling of disqualification or rejection, it may be hard for you to believe God could love you enough to show you mercy, forgive you and set you on a path of influence for Him. But if God did it for Paul, why wouldn't He do it for you? You are not a special case. As you come to Christ, He forgives you, chooses to not act upon your sin and equips you for a life of moment-by-moment ministry. That's EMPOWERING love.

PICK and PRAY

➻ Say a prayer in which you accept God's mercy and forgiveness for you.

➻ Ask God what ministry He has for you in this season of your life.

➻ What does God's empowering love look like in your life, and what does it mean to you?

PROCESS

_____

_____

_____

_____

_____

_____

_____

❧ 2 Timothy ❧
HOPEFUL LOVE

I have fought the good fight, I have finished the race, I have kept the faith. Henceforth, there is laid up for me the crown of righteousness, which the Lord, the righteous judge, will award to me on the Day, and not only to me but also to all who have loved his appearing.
2 Timothy 4:7-8

As we crack open our Bible (or Bible app) to 2 Timothy, we get the privilege of reading Paul's last letter to his protégé and "true son in the faith"[31] Timothy. I love Paul's heart as he comes to the end of his life and finds it crucial to send words of encouragement to his faithful mentee turned spiritual son turned pastor. Side note: if we have been walking with Christ long enough to have someone younger look up to us or step into a role we've been filling for years, the loving and responsible thing to do is to encourage and assist them in whatever way we can. It's an easily doable contribution to the kingdom.

Go ahead and read *2 Timothy 4:1-8*.

Don't you want to get to the end of your life and be able to say with Paul that you kept the faith? That you fought the good fight – the one that matters for all of eternity?

If someone were to ask you what fight you are fighting right now, what would you say?

What about if they asked if you are keeping the faith?

I don't ask those questions to induce feelings of guilt. I ask them to make us stop and look at what life we're living – whether it's the one that matters the most to us.

Paul peers out onto the fading landscape of his life and says, "I have finished the race," and dreams of the reward Christ will bestow on him when He returns to this sodden earth on the Last Day to retrieve His faithful ones. Whether that reward is an actual crown of some sort, or the "crown" is righteousness itself we do not know.[32] However, we know it is the hope to which Paul looks forward. He has no doubt in his mind that his life lived fully committed to a radical walk with Christ will be worth it. He's endured all manner of suffering – from numerous shipwrecks to snake bites – but he's also witnessed hordes of people coming into life-saving faith in the true Messiah Jesus Christ. We can hear his peace as he gazes at all his years and sighs with satisfaction that it was all worth it.

God asks His people to do some funky things. Shoot, he's asked me to spend my life pursuing relationships with people who weren't even born when I was graduating from college! He also won't allow us to buy a house and has had us rent for almost our entire marriage. It's countercultural, and I'm sure loads of people our own age think us immature dreamers. However, when we live our lives in obedience to the weird or difficult things, we, like Paul, will be able to look death in the face with peace knowing our life was well-spent. We will be confident as we look forward to the reward of Christ awaiting us. That's HOPEFUL love.

PICK and PRAY

➥ In what way can you keep the faith? Fight the good fight? Finish the race?

➥ Is there something countercultural or a little intimidating God is asking you to do? What's keeping you from doing it? What would it look like if you obeyed?

➥ What does God's hopeful love look like in your life, and what does it mean to you?

PROCESS

✎ Titus ✎

ETERNAL LOVE

For the grace of God has appeared,
bringing salvation for all people
Titus 2:11

I am the master of grand ideas and fabulous beginnings. Big dreams and enthusiastic kick-offs. I've sold supplements, plastic bowls, bags, and electricity in an effort to make my work-from-home aspirations a reality. Burpable lid, anyone? But the middle. The middle always gets me. My excitement wanes in the mucky middle where tenacity is required. I just can't muster that kind of passion for kitchenware, man. I'm glad that, again, Jesus is nothing like me in this regard.

Take a minute and read *Titus 2:11-14*.

Grace. Sometimes we rush over that word because it is written so often in the Bible. I don't want us to do that today. It's a beautiful word.

Grace

"good will, loving-kindness, favour . . . of the merciful kindness by
which God, exerting his holy influence upon souls, turns them to
Christ, keeps, strengthens, increases them in Christian faith,
knowledge, affection, and kindles them to the exercise of the
Christian virtues"[33]

What is your favorite part of that definition? Would you highlight or underline it?

What is it about that part that draws you to it?

Now take that word or phrase and picture Jesus accomplishing it for you every single day of your life. Make it personal. That truth is not just for the people we believe may deserve it more than we do. No one deserves it; it's unmerited. It's for them, and it's for you.

If you notice in both our definition and our scripture portion, grace is not a one-time action Jesus performed on the cross. He didn't gift us salvation and then leave us to our own devices to figure out the rest. He not only woos us to Himself, He trains us to walk with Him and to endure patiently with trust, strengthens us for the good works He has prepared for us to do, and increases our faith, knowledge and love. Grace is ongoing. Grace is active. Grace is every day.

And I am sure of this, that he who began a good work in you will
bring it to completion at the day of Jesus Christ.
(Php. 1:6)

Many love stories end in abandonment. One partner starts to falter somewhere in the middle of the plot, and the book closes with the other staring off into the sunset as love rides away. Bang up beginning, mediocre middle and a failure of an end. But the greatest love story of all – the one featuring you and your bridegroom Jesus – doesn't have a final chapter. The story goes on into eternity and gets better with every chapter. Jesus, the hero of your story, sees you through every season, strengthening you and encouraging you along the way, until He sweeps you off your feet and carries you straight into the Father's arms. That's ETERNAL love.

PICK and PRAY

➻ How can you accept God's grace more today? How can you show it to others?

➻ Have you ever thought of Jesus as your groom? Picture that and process.

➻ What does God's eternal love look like in your life, and what does it mean to you?

PROCESS

∂ Philemon ∾

TANGIBLE LOVE

*For I have derived much joy and comfort from your love, my
brother, because the hearts of the saints have been
refreshed through you.*
Philemon 1:7

Another letter from Paul. It's astounding that the same man who harbored such violent hatred for Christians ended up composing the majority of the New Testament and speaking of Christ followers like he does in this epistle: with unselfish love. Only God can do that in a life.

Paul was a spiritual giant of a trailblazer and led thousands of people to the feet of Christ, but there must have been days when he suffered in spirit. He couldn't have been strong every day of his life. Recently, I became aware of the marriage separation of a woman in ministry who many people consider a spiritual giant as well. I'm sure she would refute that term because, as far as I can tell, she is super humble. When the news broke of her husband's infidelity, I remember thinking, *What? I can't believe that could happen to her!* I wondered if she had the support she needed to hold her up during such a crushing season. Leadership can be a lonely place sometimes. We found out later she did indeed have friends and family to help, and her husband must have too since there has been a beautiful reconciliation and healing in their marriage.

Reading this letter to Philemon, I can't help but consider whether or not he was such a friend to Paul. We can't be sure how deep their relationship ran (Phil was somewhere near Colossae or Laodicia and Paul in Rome)[34], but we can hear the love and concern Paul has for Philemon and Onesimus, the friend about whom Paul is writing. Go ahead and read *Philemon 1*.

Why do you think Paul calls Onesimus his child in verse 10?

It sounds like Paul introduced Onesimus to a relationship with Christ while they were both in prison. Even while being held in chains, Paul is so in love with God and His people that he can't help but tell everyone about the hope and salvation they can have. That's a convicting word right there!

Paul goes on to plead for hospitality for his new convert and to express his desire to return to Philemon's city to see him. We can clearly feel his affection for them both. If we step back and observe the contents of this letter with a wider lens, we see God using His people to support, comfort and love their brothers.

115

Paul – expresses love and concern for Onesimus and Philemon, secures safety for his friend and speaks of a group of fellow kingdom workers

Philemon – described as having love toward God and his church and shares the gospel faithfully

These men are supporting each other, taking care of one another and comforting when needed. This is how God works – through other people. Sometimes we want the big moment or the miracle, but that miracle comes wrapped in human flesh most of the time. *We* are the hands and feet of Jesus. He uses us to actively care for each other. That's TANGIBLE love.

PICK and PRAY

➤➤ Thank God for anyone who has shown His love to you.

➤➤ To whom can you be a relational manifestation of God's love?

➤➤ What does God's tangible love look like in your life, and what does it mean to you?

PROCESS

❧ Hebrews ❧

NOURISHING LOVE

looking to Jesus, the founder and perfecter of our faith
from Hebrews 12:2

I recently subscribed to a dinner service. Have you heard of these? You download the app, scroll through the week's meal offerings, select the ones you would like to cook, and a box full of all the pre-measured ingredients shows up on your door ready for you to create culinary magic. It's been a Godsend because, try as I might, I come up wanting in the area of palatable meal creation about 80% of the time. I simply don't know how to put flavors together to produce yum. Every Tuesday when I hear that box dropped on my front porch, I dance a jig because it's creating something for me I just can't do myself.

According to *Hebrews 12:1-2*, who is the author (creator) and perfecter of our faith?

What does it mean to be an author?

What about a perfecter?

There is much talk in the Bible and church about faith. We learn in the 11th chapter of Hebrews that we cannot please God without it. So, we know it is an integral part of our lives with God.

What do you think faith means?

Strong's Exhaustive Concordance defines it as *trust, belief, confidence* or *faithfulness*.[35] As believers we want to trust and believe what God says and have confidence enough in Him to be faithful. That's faith, and practicing it is a mighty tall order. However, what makes these verses so beautiful is they explain that we're not meant to manufacture our faith, so we are free to stop trying.

We are simply not able to do it.

An author fashions original words on a page, and Jesus does the same for our belief. It comes from Him, not us. Much like my inability to look in my pantry and produce a meal, we are, quite frankly, unable to create faith. We can't *make* ourselves believe.

We also can't grow our faith to maturity. Yes, we can learn more about God and get to know Him better through His word and prayer, but according to this verse, it is Jesus who makes our faith whole and mature. We make ourselves available to Him, and Jesus perfects our faith.

This takes off some pressure, doesn't it? It relieves some shame we might have over some areas of doubt, right? Take heart. Our job is not to force ourselves into faith; it is to surrender to Jesus' activity in our lives. Then, as we lean into Him, he will lovingly feed and cultivate our faith in such a way that we are able to run the race He has placed before us. That's NOURISHING love.

PICK and PRAY

➻ How has God grown your faith recently?

➻ Thank God that you don't have the power to make yourself believe more.

➻ What does God's nourishing love look like in your life, and what does it mean to you?

PROCESS

❧ *James* ❧

STABILIZING LOVE

*If any of you lacks wisdom, let him ask God, who gives generously
to all without reproach, and it will be given him.*
James 1:5

I try to be reverent; I really do. It's important in our relationship with God, especially in these times when it seems so many people's picture of God has become small and wimpy. I want to be honoring in my tone, so please hear what I'm about to say through that filter. The beginning of James chapter one has always been difficult for me. I can even go as far as to say I have hated verses two and three. Maybe it's because people have flippantly thrown these verses at me while I'm in the midst of deep suffering just trying to figure out how to trust God again. I don't know. Go ahead and read *James 1:1-18* and see what you think.

Now that I'm more healed, I'm able to read past those first three verses and see the value of suffering.

What does suffering produce?

Perseverance is good. So is maturity. We also get the crown of life and good gifts from God Himself. Those are hopeful promises when we are slogging through trials we feel cemented in.

Take a look at 1:5-8. These verses almost seem out of place as James suddenly begins discussing wisdom. However, when we put it in context, we see he is speaking about our need for wisdom in our times of trial. I don't know about you, but I never feel more lost than when I am mucking through difficulty. In the midst of suffering, when every single drop of our energy seems to be routed to keeping us from drowning, decision-making becomes almost impossible. We often find ourselves wondering, *What do I do?* James has the answer.

In verse 5, what does James say to do when we need wisdom?

Seems so simple, doesn't it? Ask God for your next step – for clarity. God is not a God of confusion.[36] He wants to help. Look again for God's response to our asking for that wisdom.

How does He give? To whom?

He's willing to give wisdom to anyone who asks, and He gives it generously. He's not holding out on us or making us jump through hoops to hear from Him. Sometimes He's simply waiting for us to ask. We request wisdom, and He gives it – without shaming us. Thank you, Lord.

Here's the rub though. We cannot doubt His answers or we "won't receive anything from the Lord" and will be "like a wave of the sea that is driven and tossed by the wind." Note: God is not saying that He can see us doubting, so He's going to withhold the wisdom. This one is on us. He may be answering, but if we doubt what He's saying, we're unable to receive the wisdom. It doesn't say if we doubt He stops giving. It says we stop receiving. It's an unbelief problem.

God loves us. He never wants us to suffer alone, and He provides answers, gifts and wisdom in the middle of our most trying times. I pray today we are able to receive His wisdom without doubt. Then we will no longer be as the wild waves of the ocean but like a steady ship tethered to our strong Anchor. That's STABILIZING love.

PICK and PRAY

➤ What do you need to ask God wisdom for today?

➤ When has God given you wisdom in the past? How can that encourage you for the future?

➤ What does God's stabilizing love look like in your life, and what does it mean to you?

PROCESS

❧ 1 Peter ❧

WORTH-BESTOWING LOVE

As you come to him, a living stone rejected by men but in the sight of God chosen and precious, you yourselves like living stones are being built up as a spiritual house, to be a holy priesthood, to offer spiritual sacrifices acceptable to God through Jesus Christ.
1 Peter 2:4-5

When I graduated from college, my mom hooked me up with an interview with the Fortune 500 company at which she worked. It was my first real adult job interview, so I sprinted right over to my older sister's house to raid her closet filled with professional attire. I gazed in the mirror to behold my 5' 5" frame looking like a child playing dress up in her 5' 9" mom's clothing and wondered if I had what it took to make it at a "real" job. As I sat in the Human Resources Director's office and shot off rehearsed answers to her questions, I relaxed. She seemed to genuinely enjoy me, and we parted with her pat on the back and smile at the end of our time together. I landed that job somehow. My suspicion is my mom leveraged her relationship with the interviewer. I didn't care as long as I got the position. As I set up my new workspace in a small cubicle on my first day, I couldn't believe I was given the responsibility of this job. I felt honored. Excited and looking forward to the future. But as the months rolled by, my fervor started to wane. I began every morning by peeling myself out of bed, reluctant to face another day at the office. About month eight, I realized a desk job was not what I was made to do. Ashamed, I turned in my two weeks' notice and left that wonderful, well-paying job to return to waiting tables. Now what? What was I supposed to be doing with this hard-earned college degree? I felt lost.

If I had only known Jesus back then, I would have found such comfort in our scripture portion today. Go ahead and read *1 Peter 2:1-12*.

The living stone rejected by men but chosen and precious to the Father that Peter is referring to here is Jesus. That description can preach on its own about our worth being found in God only, but that's a different discussion for a different study. What I want to settle on is verse five. Living stones – it's what we are too, and we are also being built up as a spiritual house and a holy priesthood. These are powerful roles.

Spiritual House – We are the church. You. Me. All believers are making up a home that is to be a welcoming, truth-filled place of worship for *anyone* who wishes to enter.

Holy Priesthood – This one stops me cold. The priesthood was a position held by very few, and it had strict requirements and responsibilities. It was a role of honor

121

in which the priest served the people by presenting daily sacrifices and prayers on their behalf. A priesthood position is a big deal.

These are the privileges we receive when we decide to accept Jesus' gift of grace. Whether we are alone or in a group, we carry the church into every nook and cranny of society. *This* is our real job, no matter what our occupation may be.

We get to be a place of welcome, love and truth for everyone we meet. We all become priests in that we worship God, pray for and serve others and sacrifice our will for God's. We live our lives for Him in order that others "may see [our] good deeds and glorify God".[37] What an honor it is to be given a position that has the potential to change the eternity of the people around us. We need never feel insignificant again. God not only saved us; He gave us a job and a life of purpose and value. That's WORTH-BESTOWING love.

PICK and PRAY

➤➤ How does being the church and a priest make you feel? Submit those feeling to God.

➤➤ Who took their role as a priest seriously and reached you for Christ? Thank God for them.

➤➤ What does God's worth-bestowing love look like in your life, and what does it mean to you?

PROCESS

_____

_____

_____

_____

_____

_____

_____

_____

✍ 2 Peter ✍

PATIENT LOVE

The Lord is not slow to fulfill his promise as some count slowness,
but is patient toward you, not wishing that any should perish, but
that all should reach repentance.
2 Peter 3:9

Have you ever had one of those days when you just wanted to say to Jesus, "I'm cool with you returning today. I'm done with this world and all its craziness. Go ahead and come on back"? Sometimes the pressures we face, whether during a particularly difficult time or in the normal, daily grind, can make us want to quit. We wonder why God lets this world keep on turning with all the evil and sadness we see swirling around it. On the home page of our local news station today alone there are two murder stories and a burglary bust. When we see that kind of thing, we can get weighed down with the negative and begin to believe the world is beyond help. It's then that we are at risk of checking out of life to just survive until we die or Jesus returns.

That's no way to live.

Go ahead and read *2 Peter 3:8-13*, please.

"The day of the Lord" refers to that day when this world will cease to exist and Jesus will come back to claim His children and usher in a new Heaven and Earth over which He will reign. If that sounds kinda nutty to you, remember that He has already created the ground on which you stand. Long ago, He fashioned fuzzy creatures of all shapes and sizes and knitted every human together with all our complex DNA and cell structure. Doing it again is no big whoop. When Jesus returns, it will be a time of no more pain or tears or sadness. It will be breathtakingly awesome. And we will have solace as we dwell in the direct presence of the Prince of Peace.

"So, what are we waiting for, then?" you might be asking. Read our focus verse one more time. The promise referred to there is the promise of His return. According to this verse, why is He slow in keeping that promise?

God is beyond the restrictions of time. Isn't that a hinky thing to think about? He is everywhere all at once. He created the sun and moon that rule our daytime schedules and seasons. He is outside of time and present in eternity. Therefore, as we wonder why it's taking so long for Jesus to return and put an end to all this evil in our world, it's just a blink of the eye to Him.

123

He's beyond us, and I'm so grateful our God can't be contained.

Though a thousand years is like a day to God, the fact is, He is waiting until just the right time to come back. He wants *none* to perish. His heart is that every single person He has created will choose Him, and He wants to give them every chance to do it.

Right now, who is someone you could pray for to come into a relationship with Him during this time He is waiting?

Jesus longs for us all to turn to Him and be saved. He waits until the very last person He knows will choose Him does so. That is PATIENT love.

PICK and PRAY

➤➤ Write down the name of the person you're praying for somewhere you will see it often.

➤➤ Thank God for waiting for *you* to give your heart to Him.

➤➤ What does God's patient love look like in your life, and what does it mean to you?

PROCESS

_____

_____

_____

_____

_____

_____

_____

_____

_____

☙ 1 John ❧

DEPENDABLE LOVE

So we have come to know and to believe the love that God has for
us. God is love, and whoever abides in love abides in God,
and God abides in him.
1 John 4:16

If a new friend were to ask you to describe yourself, to tell her who you are, what would you say?

These are the times I wish you and I were chummy neighbors with nothing to do but brew some local snooty coffee and chat over a breakfast item with the caloric count of an entire vat of fried chicken. I so badly want to hear your answer. Ooh! Send it to me on Instagram! Since a face-to-face breakfast date isn't a thing for us, I'll just tell you what I would probably say, and you get to have all the fun, okay? I'm an obsessive overthinker. I'm sappy and sassy with a side of middle-aged boho. On a really good day, I'm a bit funny. Also, I'm a cat lady who is, in fact, allergic to cats. I am quite literally a cat whisperer who can charm the most frustrating feline into a furry roly-poly asking for tummy rubs, but I will then descend into the abyss of snot and sneeze. What in all the fur balls was God doing when He created that combination? Alas, His ways are higher than mine.

Go ahead and read *1 John 4:7-21*.

Were you thinking there would be a cat in there somewhere? Nah, but there's still good stuff to be found. Up to this point in this book we've been talking all about the different ways God shows us He loves us. We've seen Him forgive us, sing over us, delight in us, and fight for us, just to name a few. Do a quick little look-back at all our entries to date. What are a couple of ways God loves us that impact you most and you want to make sure you remember?

Tuck those away somewhere you can review them, and then take a look at our focus scripture today. You'll notice the beginning of that second sentence begins with *God is love*.

God **is** love.

Not God *has* love. God *is* love. It's who He is. If someone were to ask us to describe Jesus – to tell them who He is – we could safely answer that He is love.

You may be wondering what the difference between having love and being love is. Let me give you a very Misti-type example. Do you agree there is a difference between *having* a donut and *being* a donut? If I have a donut, I'm free to act on having it by eating it or not eating it. I can even discard it – throw it out. Maybe I have a kolache instead. However, if I *am* a donut, I have no other choice but to act out of being a donut. I can't act like a kolache if I'm a donut. Well, maybe the analogy gets a little weird right there, but you get it.

God is love. He can never act out of a different nature because He doesn't possess one. He will never *not* be compassionate or forgiving or attentive. He is love, so every single thing He does towards us is loving – even if, in our limited understanding, something doesn't seem loving. He will never *not* love you or love you less. If we use that as our filter, there ain't no shakin' us no matter what God lets in our life. Love is who He is, and that never changes. That's DEPENDABLE love.

PICK and PRAY

➡ What would change in your life if you could live out of the truth that God is always love?

➡ Talk to God and journal about one of your answers above.

➡ What does God's dependable love look like in your life, and what does it mean to you?

PROCESS

๛ 2 John ๛

ABUNDANT LOVE

Grace, mercy, and peace will be with us, from God the Father and
from Jesus Christ the Father's Son, in truth and love.
2 John 1:3

My nickname in junior high was Spaz. I think at one point it was meant to be derogatory – because preteens – but somewhere along the way I became fond of the name and wore it proudly. There was even a weekend my little group of friends called The Crew (don't you love the adolescent need to label everything) made boxer short bloomers emblazoned with our nicknames in puffy paint. So, for about a year I periodically walked around in islet lace-trimmed underwear with Spaz written on the butt. Painted underwear as outerwear. What even?

Though my body calmed as I aged, my mind did not. It raced with worry, fear, perfectionism and ambition. It still does sometimes, and after talking with many women, I know I'm not alone.

Does your mind ever race? What are the thoughts that are whizzing around your brain at times like that?

Thankfully, truths like the ones found in *2 John 1:1-3* can quiet our whirling thoughts quickly. Go ahead and give it a read.

Grace, mercy and peace. We need a hefty helping of those every day to keep our running thoughts at rest. As we discussed in Titus, grace is a wonderful gift, and when you add mercy and peace, it just gets better.

The Bible Knowledge Commentary highlights the core, original meanings of these words beautifully: "favor", "compassion" and "inner harmony and tranquility".[38]

Grace/Favor – You are God's favorite. And so am I. He is always on our side and causing us to have favor with others who are part of His plan for us.

Mercy/Compassion – Many people see God as a dictator out to police and punish us. His heart is actually to love and bless us. He is out to love you, not harm you.

Peace/Inner harmony and tranquility – We just feel our shoulders lighten when we consider God's ability and desire to calm us. He wants to kill the chaos and overrun our busy brains with peace.

Did you notice that these refreshing gifts come directly from God the Father and from Jesus Christ? John goes so far as to say we *will* have them when we are "in" truth and love. Sounds like a promise to me.

So what is the truth and love we are meant to be "in"? In John 14:6, Jesus calls Himself the Truth, and we just learned in 1 John that He is also love. So, Jesus is the truth and love, and if we continue to put ourselves in a position to be with Him, the reward is grace, mercy and peace. He is the source of it all.

Our world is filled with criticism, judgment and frenzy. Compassion and tranquility are tough to come by. But in this culture of chaos, God whispers, "Be still. Shut out the world for just a bit and sit with me." It's in those moments when we are eye-deep in His word that He showers us with the grace, mercy and peace we so desperately need. That's ABUNDANT love.

PICK and PRAY

➤➤ How can you put yourself in a place to be with Jesus today?

➤➤ Does grace, mercy or peace mean more to you in this present season? Why?

➤➤ What does God's abundant love look like in your life, and what does it mean to you?

PROCESS

ᴏᴗ 3 John ᴗᴄ

TRANSFORMATIVE LOVE

I have no greater joy than to hear that my children are walking in the truth.
3 John 1:4

Please read *3 John 1* looking for John's attitude toward his friend Gaius. Give your best guess as to how he feels about him.

It's nice to hear a man speak to a friend with such words of kindness, isn't it? I'm sometimes saddened by the pressure we put on our menfolk to "man up". There's just something refreshing about a man who is comfortable expressing his feelings. I suppose it's my obsession with freedom and security to be who God made you to be, but that's neither here nor there.

What does Philippians 1:6 say God will continue to do until the day of Jesus Christ?

God begins a work in us the minute we start walking with Him – before that, really, since He is the One who woos us into a relationship with Him before we even know He's calling. He then continues to "work out our salvation", or sanctify us, for the rest of our lives. That's just fancy church talk to describe how God continues to heal us and make us more like Jesus every day. He lovingly turns us away from the things that hurt us and hurt others. He addresses and heals the parts of us that keep us at a distance from Him and develops all the qualities in us that look like his Son.

When I read John's letter to Gaius, I can't help but notice evidence that God has done exactly that in his life.

- He calls Gaius *beloved* four times in the span of 11 verses. When God, who is love, begins to take us over, we splash it out on those around us.
- He rejoiced when he heard how his "child" Gaius was walking in truth. When God, who is truth, begins to take us over, we are overjoyed as someone is freed by that truth.

- He commends Gaius for supporting their brothers in the faith. When God, who is the giver of life and every perfect gift, begins to take us over, we can't help but give out of the overflow of gifts we've received.
- He longs to spend time with Gaius face-to-face. When God, who is the ultimate friend, begins to take us over, we walk out of our isolation toward the people around us.

God is in the business of renewing us. You may have heard the cliché "God loves you just the way you are but too much to leave you that way." As trite as that statement is, it holds deep truth. There is nothing about us that is so repulsive to God that it would make Him not love us. He has looked at our most disgusting sin, grabbed us up and loved us into His kingdom. But His love doesn't stop there. He continues in such close, active relationship with us that if we continually respond to Him, we begin to look more and more like Him every day. That's TRANSFORMATIVE love.

PICK and PRAY

➻ How have you seen God begin and continue His good work in you? Thank Him.

➻ What one area would you like to ask God to lovingly transform you to look more like Jesus?

➻ What does God's transformative love look like in your life today, and what does it mean to you?

PROCESS

❧ Jude ❧

PROTECTIVE LOVE

To those who are called, beloved in God the Father and kept for
Jesus Christ: May mercy, peace, and love be multiplied to you.
from Jude 1:1-2

Sometimes I just like to hear good things about myself. I may ask my husband how I look in my new jeans just to hear how he finds me attractive. Or when I'm feeling dreary, I might call my mom so she can gush about how fabulous I am. There are days when we just need to hear the nice things.

Our scripture portion is small today, but there's a sweet nugget in there for you. If you're feeling over-achieverish, read the whole book. At one chapter, it'll only take a few minutes. If you're in a bit more of a hurry, feel happy with simply reading *Jude 1:1-2*.

Jude is a good read, but I get stopped right at the greeting. Although he is writing to an ancient reader, the qualities Jude uses to describe them apply to us too, since we are also God's people.

Let's look at them. What's the first thing you think when you hear these words used to describe you?

Called –

Beloved –

Kept –

My favorite is *kept*. I could sit there for a spell, but all three are wonderful. The following explanations come from our understanding of the ancient Greek in which they were written.

Called – "called, invited (to a banquet); invited (by God in the proclamation of the Gospel) to obtain eternal salvation in the kingdom through Christ"[39]

Beloved – "the deep and constant 'love' and interest of a perfect Being towards entirely unworthy objects, producing and fostering a reverential 'love' in them towards the Giver, and a practical 'love' towards those who are partakers of the same, and a desire to help others to seek the Giver."[40]

131

Kept – "to attend to carefully, take care of; to guard; metaph. to keep, one in the state in which he is; to observe; to reserve: to undergo something"[41]

Underline any part you particularly like in the definitions. Because God loves us deeply and constantly, He *invites* us into a saving relationship with Him. Invited. It's the best to be invited to an exclusive event, isn't it? However, I'm thankful the invitation into Jesus' family isn't just for an elite few. He wants everyone to come into a relationship with Him.[42] *You* are invited. *You* are His beloved.

And you are kept. God watches over you, guarding and protecting you every step of every day. There is never a moment when He is not walking with you carefully attending your way. What a humbling thought. We are the beloved of the Most High whom He woos lovingly and shelters endlessly. That's PROTECTIVE love.

PICK and PRAY

➤ Which one of the bolded adjectives means the most to you? Why?

➤ What was the difference between your definition and the original definitions of the words? How is that significant?

➤ What does God's protective love look like in your life, and what does it mean to you?

PROCESS

_____

_____

_____

_____

_____

_____

_____

_____

_____

❧ Revelation ❧
INCLUSIVE LOVE

*The Spirit and the Bride say, "Come." And let the one who hears
say, "Come." And let the one who is thirsty come; let the one who
desires take the water of life without price.*
Revelation 22:17

Usually, when you come to the last chapter of a book, you've hit the end. There is no more story to tell. You might feel a sense of accomplishment or a sense of relief it's finally over. You may be satisfied with the ending or left disappointed because you spent the last month reading something that ended poorly. There's nothing worse in the literature world than a lackluster finish. No matter what emotions you experience at the completion of a book, the one all people can agree they feel is an awareness that it's over. They are done. However, as we read the last chapter of the final book of our Bible, we realize we haven't come to the end. Take a look, one last time, at your scripture portion for today: *Revelation 22:16-17*.

What 3 ways is Jesus characterized in verse 16?

Which one interests you the most? Why?

Though I love all three descriptions, I am all about new beginnings. You can't beat the joy and anticipation of leaving something difficult behind and forging ahead into something new and hopeful. Jesus being called the bright morning star reminds us that what He ushers in at the end of the age will be new and nothing but light and life.

What word is repeated over and over again in verse 17?

It's a beautiful sentiment to end our time together, isn't it?

Come. Tell everyone else to come too.

Jesus sometimes gets a bad rap because people feel His teaching that we can only be saved by accepting Him is exclusive. In other words, only Christians get salvation. While it may be true that the only way to the Father is through Jesus[43], we see right here that the invitation is open to anybody.

Absolutely anyone.

The penthouse dweller and the underpass sleeper. The priest and the prostitute. He is no respecter of persons; His heart beats for us all.

We have spent 66 days imbibing God's multi-faceted love. He wants us to get it and live out of that love every day. But He also says, "Let the one who hears say, 'Come.'" That's you and me. We have heard for the last two months. Now it is time for us to communicate God's love to those around us – to let them know they are invited into a relationship with the God who deeply loves every single one of us and excludes no one. That's INCLUSIVE love.

PICK and PRAY

➤➤ Who will you love like Jesus today? Is there someone who needs to know they're included?

➤➤ Thank Jesus for including you and dying for *you* so that you could be included too.

➤➤ What does God's inclusive love look like in your life today, and what does it mean to you?

PROCESS

_____

_____

_____

_____

_____

_____

_____

_____

_____

_____

a final note from misti

I feel like we are friends by this point, don't you? I hope these last 66 (or however many) days unearthing the treasure of God's heart for you has moved you closer to believing His love for you personally. If you're not quite there, it's okay. Faith is a journey, not a destination. Don't accept any shame at all. Celebrate your small steps. You believe more today than you did when we began this adventure together. That's worth celebrating! Just keep praying God would daily open your eyes to how much He loves you. He's faithful. He'll show up.

If it's okay with you, I'd like to have our last moments together be some time spent talking to this God who loves us in such incredibly diverse ways.

Jesus, you are the Lover of our souls. We hear that over and over again in the church, but help us to embrace it for ourselves. To believe it so deeply that we can't help but live our lives out of that truth. Thank you for these days spent imbibing your unashamed, fully present and active love for us. May we never lose sight of it or start believing we are anything but ferociously adored by you. We are your daughters. We are cherished, and we are valued . . . simply because you say so. Thank you. We know the price you paid was high, and we are so grateful. Strengthen us to stay grounded in your compassion and pour it out on others. We love you, amen.

You are His beloved. Walk in it.

❧ Appendix: How To Look Up Scripture ❧

The Bible is composed of 66 separate books. It can get a tad daunting when someone tells you to find one little bitty scripture in that big, honking book. Here's some help.

1. When you see something like: Colossians 4:2, you have come upon a "scripture reference". It tells you exactly where to find the scripture in the Bible.
2. First, locate the name of the book you're looking for in the Table of Contents at the front of your Bible. For instance, if I'm searching for Colossians 4:2, I will look for "Colossians" in the Table of Contents. Turn to that page.
3. Once you've found the book, you will need to locate the chapter of the scripture. The chapter is the first number listed in the scripture reference. In Colossians 4:2, the chapter number is 4, so we need to find chapter 4. Chapter numbers are the big, sometimes bolded, numbers in scripture.
4. When you're at the big 4, it's time to search out the tiny scripture number. In Colossians 4:2, we are looking for verse 2. These numbers are noted within the text and are smaller, so you will have to look closer to find them. Boom! You found Colossians 4:2!

❧ Notes ❧

Exodus

[1] "Exodus 3-4." *Verse By Verse Ministry of San Antonio,*
   https://www.versebyverseministry.org/images/uploads/exodus_3-4.pdf.
Accessed
   2 February 2019.

Leviticus

[2] Leviticus 4

Judges

[3] Constable, Dr. Thomas L. "Notes of Judges 2017 Edition." *Plano Bible Chapel,*
   https://www.planobiblechapel.org/tcon/notes/html/ot/judges/judges.htm.
   Accessed 3 February 2019.

Judges

[4] Romans 8:38 - 39
[5] 1 Corinthians 1:28 - 29
[6] Ephesians 1:5
[7] Luke 12:6 - 7
[8] 2 Timothy 1:7
[9] Isaiah 55:1 – 3

1 Kings

[10] 1 Chronicles 28:3

Ezra

[11] Wright, Paul H. *Rose Then and Now Bible Map Atlas: with Biblical
   Background and Culture.* Edited by Barbara L. Ball, (Carson, CA: Rose
   Publishing Inc, 2013), 7.

[12] Ibid, 118-119.

Nehemiah

[13] "Young Life Camp Properties." *Young Life,*
   https://camp.younglife.org/Pages/Young-Life-Camp-Properties.aspx. Accessed 7
   February 2019.

[14] Wright, Paul H. *Rose Then and Now Bible Map Atlas: with Biblical
   Background and Culture.* Edited by Barbara L. Ball, (Carson, CA: Rose
   Publishing Inc, 2013), 123.

Psalms

[15] Keller, W. Phillip. *A Shepherd Looks at Psalm 23*. (Grand Rapids, MI: Zondervan, 2015), chapter 5.

Isaiah

[16] Dyer, Charles H., et al. *Old Testament Explorer: Discovering the Essence, Background, and Meaning of Every Book in the Old Testament*. (Word Publishing, 2001), 527.

Lamentations

[17] Foster, Jeremy. "Trailblazers Part 2." Hope City Church. Houston, TX. 13 January 2019. Sermon.

[18] *Blue Letter Bible*. https://www.blueletterbible.org/lang/lexicon/lexicon.cfm?Strongs=H7227&t= ESV. Accessed 14 February 2019.

[19] Romans 8:38

Joel

[20] Hebrews 12:6
[21] Romans 8:37
[22] 2 Corinthians 10:4

Micah

[23] "The Book of Micah". *Illustrated Dictionary & Concordance of the Bible*. (The Reader's Digest Association, Inc., with the permission of GG. The Jerusalem Publishing House Ltd., 1986), 688.

Haggai

[24] Alexander, Pat and David. *Zondervan Handbook to the Bible*. (Oxford, England: Lion Publishing plc, 1999), 505.

Zechariah

[25] Ibid, 507.

Galatians

[26] Campbell, Donald K. "Galatians". *The New Testament Bible Knowledge Commentary*, edited by John F. Walvoord and Roy B.Zuck, (SP Publishing, 1983), 597.

Colossians
[27] Colossians 1:16

1 Timothy
[28] Acts 9
[29] Galatians 2:11-14
[30] Acts 15:36-40

2 Timothy
[31] 1 Timothy 1:2

[32] Litfin, A. Duane. "2 Timothy". *The New Testament Bible Knowledge Commentary*, edited by John F. Walvoord and Roy B.Zuck, (SP Publishing, 1983), 758.

Titus
[33] *Blue Letter Bible.*
   https://www.blueletterbible.org/lang/lexicon/lexicon.cfm?Strongs=G5485&t=ESV. Accessed 20 February 2019.

Philemon
[34] "Epistle to Philemon". *Illustrated Dictionary & Concordance of the Bible*. (The Reader's Digest Association, Inc., with the permission of GG. The Jerusalem Publishing House Ltd., 1986), 784.

Hebrews
[35] *Blue Letter Bible.*
   https://www.blueletterbible.org/lang/lexicon/lexicon.cfm?Strongs=G4102&t=ESV. Accessed 21 February 2019.

James
[36] 1 Corinthians 14:33

1 Peter
[37] 1 Peter 2:12

[38] Raymer, Roger M. "1 Peter". *The New Testament Bible Knowledge Commentary,*
   edited by John F. Walvoord and Roy B.Zuck, (SP Publishing, 1983), 906.

Jude

[39] *Blue Letter Bible.*
https://www.blueletterbible.org/lang/lexicon/lexicon.cfm?Strongs=G2822&t=
ESV. Accessed 22 February 2019.

[40] *Blue Letter Bible.*
https://www.blueletterbible.org/lang/lexicon/lexicon.cfm?Strongs=G25&t=
ESV. Accessed 22 February 2019.

[41] *Blue Letter Bible.*
https://www.blueletterbible.org/lang/lexicon/lexicon.cfm?Strongs=G5083&t=
ESV. Accessed 22 February 2019.

[42] 2 Peter 3:9

Revelation

[43] John 14:6

Made in the USA
Monee, IL
26 April 2020